4|21|17
$2995

ELEGANT
SOUTACHE

ELEGANT
SOUTACHE

Amee K. Sweet-McNamara

LARK
New York

This book is dedicated to the Wise Women of the
family into which I was lucky enough to be born.

To the memory of Grandma Betty, who introduced me to decorative
furniture painting, flower arranging, and hand-drawn paper dolls.

To the memory of my Great Aunt Pearl, who shared her love of
doll making, embellished eggs, and glitter.

To my Aunt Kris, who gave me my first sewing basket.

And to my mother, Donna. Thank you, Mom—every good thing
I've ever done or ever will do is because of you.

New York

An Imprint of Sterling Publishing Co., Inc.
1166 Avenue of the Americas
New York, NY 10036

Text and step-by-step photography © 2016 by Amee K. Sweet-McNamara
Beauty shot photography © 2016 by Sterling Publishing Co., Inc.

ISBN 978-1-4547-0917-6

Distributed in Canada by Sterling Publishing Co., Inc.
c/o Canadian Manda Group, 664 Annette Street
Toronto, Ontario, Canada M6S 2C8
Distributed in the United Kingdom by GMC Distribution Services
Castle Place, 166 High Street, Lewes, East Sussex, England BN7 1XU
Distributed in Australia by NewSouth Books
45 Beach Street, Coogee, NSW 2034, Australia

For information about custom editions, special sales, and premium and corporate purchases,
please contact Sterling Special Sales at 800-805-5489 or specialsales@sterlingpublishing.com.

Manufactured in China

2 4 6 8 10 9 7 5 3 1

www.sterlingpublishing.com
www.larkcrafts.com

Credits: Beauty shot photography by Lynne Harty • Book interior design by Cindy Joy

CONTENTS

· ·

FOREWORD

Big, Bold, and Beautiful! Amee Sweet-McNamara delivers all three in her newest soutache book. Her work is filled with bold color and delivers on her philosophy of "Go Big or Go Home!"

You'll be taken on a design journey, allowing you to create the wonderful pieces included in this comprehensive guide to learning the art of soutache jewelry making.

In Living Color Cuff, Shimmering Sea Turtle Pendant, Crystal Coil Earrings, and The Impossible Romance Necklace are just a few of the fanciful names that match up with the unique style of art-to-wear pieces the author has created.

Amee's design repertoire includes combining soutache with a number of other mediums to achieve an eclectic collection of brooches, pendants, collars, bracelets, and earrings.

Beyond the soutache braid and the beads, Amee has worked with velvet, leather, shibori silk, metal, and fish leather to give the work a depth and richness that stands out.

Amee's long background in working with soutache is apparent as she photographically steps out all of the details that will result in perfecting the technique. This, along with a thorough explanation of all the basics, will have you creating the beautiful pieces presented here while expanding your knowledge of this versatile medium.

Beyond the basics, Amee has developed a language to give the reader a vocabulary for working with this medium. What could be more fun than learning how to make Lollipops, Koala Faces, Lasagna Stitches, Swans' Heads, and Rolling Waves?

Amee's well thought-out approach to stepping the reader through the learning process makes the book well suited for those never having tried their hand at soutache as well as those already advanced in the technique wanting to learn even more.

A gallery of Amee's soutache work provides the reader with a sense of design possibilities available to her with the many variations of this technique.

I invite you to spend time with this book perfecting the techniques put forward, exploring the bold use of color, and adding some unexpected materials to create the beautiful pieces in this book and beyond.

Marcia DeCoster, MadDesigns
Beadweaver, Teacher, Author
Lemon Grove, California

AUTHOR'S NOTE

The word *coalescence*—for me—is connected to two deeply meaningful concepts. The first involves the natural evolution of art and craft. The second has to do with the personal collection of knowledge and skills.

I think of traditional forms of art and craft as being "pure." Irrespective of whether they are deemed "fine art" (painting, drawing, sculpting, photography) or "craft" (knitting, beading, glassblowing, weaving), each is focused on the refinement and perfection of a specific technique or handling of a particular medium. Much of contemporary art and craft, however, looks to combine and recombine elements of those traditional pursuits, resulting in works that are fresh, new, and thought-provoking. In the world of fine art, examples include collage, assemblage, and multimedia art. Comparable examples of craft include scrapbooking, altered books, and art quilting. Each of these uses materials and tools typically associated with unrelated work or industry and brings them together in a new way—*coalescence*.

As a national instructor, teaching different classes has afforded me the opportunity to meet hundreds of creative, dedicated students. Over and over again, however, I hear the same story. Sometimes it's told with humor, other times with palpable concern or frustration. Creative people—on the whole—are drawn to the challenge and inspiration derived from learning new skills. But this fascination can cause others to perceive them as being "flighty" or lacking in "stick-to-it-iveness." I hear of a husband's pointed suggestion:

"Before you sign up for a class in polymer clay, don't you think it would be better to finish that afghan you started two years ago?" Or a family's collective eye-rolling as the tools from last year's fixation with scrapbooking are tidied away to make room for the small kiln needed for enameling. What I wish to convey to all people engaged on a journey of creative exploration is, "Have faith in the path—no stop along the way will be wasted."

Know that every class, every project, every time you hear yourself say, "I want to try that!" is bringing you one step closer to your ultimate creative destination. That destination may simply be a lifetime of joyous learning, the discovery of a passion for a particular craft or technique that fascinates you for decades, or the spontaneous eruption of an entirely new form born of your carefully acquired building blocks—*coalescence*.

In comparison to traditional crafts like knitting or weaving, soutache and bead embroidery is an infant in the world of fine craft. It incorporates traditional techniques such as hand-sewing and embroidery not generally associated with jewelry. Soutache is a material long connected only with textile embellishment. Combined with beads, cabochons, and other jewelry-oriented elements, however, highly textural pieces of wearable, fiber-art jewelry and accessories continue to emerge in new and exciting ways—*coalescence*.

INTRODUCTION

Elegant Soutache was designed to be a practical reference for beginner and experienced soutache and bead embroidery artists alike.

Beginners may choose to read through chapter 2 (The Basics) before attempting any of the projects, or simply dive into any of the projects in Part 3 with the confidence that each of the required skills will be called out in boldface and can be easily referenced as needed by looking them up alphabetically back in chapters 2 and 3 of Part 2. Other more-involved skills mentioned in the text are listed at the beginning of each project with a page number to make it easy to go back for a refresher. Those who are more familiar with soutache will be delighted to learn newer skills and techniques, as well as experience "aha!" moments when perusing chapter 3 (Additional Techniques) or the numerous sidebars that are scattered throughout these pages.

Each of the 13 projects included is meant to highlight a specific technique or skill. The projects can be built as written or modified to your heart's content. As an artist and instructor, nothing could make me happier than knowing that—within the pages of this book—you found seeds of inspiration that grew into your own, utterly unique creation.

To your own heart bead true.

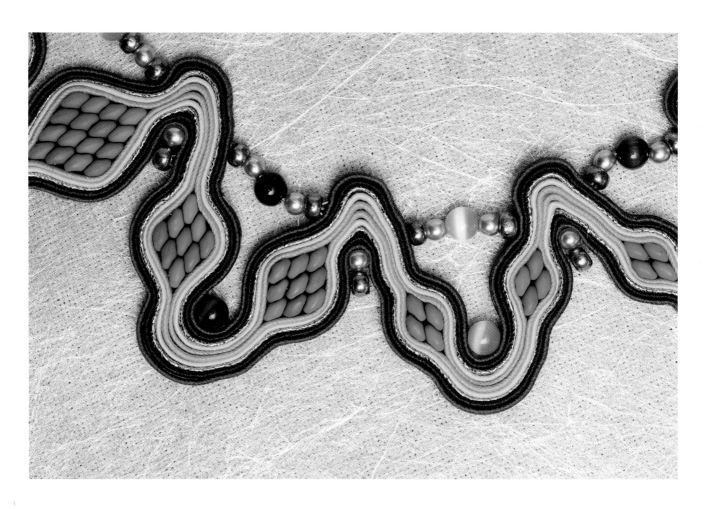

PART 1

SOUTACHE ESSENTIALS

CHAPTER 1: **MATERIALS & TOOLS**

Materials

Beading foundation. Typically available in white, beading foundation can be dyed, painted with acrylic paint, or even colored with a permanent marker to more closely match your soutache. Some manufacturers offer black and other colors. Slightly thicker beading foundation works best.

Decorative fabrics and leathers. Shibori silk, fish leather, embossed vinyl, velvet ribbon—any of these can add dramatic, textural counterpoints to your work.

Drafter's inking template. Inking templates allow you to trace basic shapes such as circles, squares, and ellipses quickly and accurately. You can find them at most large office supply stores.

Adhesives:

Jewelry glue. Designed to attach stones, glass, and plastic to metals and other materials, most brands of jewelry glue are toxic, a little messy, and harden to such a degree that it can be difficult—if not impossible—to sew through it after drying. I use this type of product only when an additional mechanical bond (such as a peyote-stitch bezel, page 57) is not possible because of the size or design of the cabochon.

Cyanoacrylate glue. Commonly known as superglue, this is available in a gel formulation and is great for attaching kumihimo end caps.

Washable fabric glue. This is my workhorse glue. There are different brands available, but look for one that is nontoxic, water-soluble while still wet, and—for the most part—behaves like the good old-fashioned white glue we all used in school. Unlike heavy-duty jewelry glues, it remains flexible after it dries, so you can still run a needle through it. This type of glue also cures (see manufacturer's label for cure times), so the finished work can actually be hand-washed with soap and water—an important consideration when creating work that is essentially a textile.

Soutache. Soutache is braid made up of fine fibers wrapped figure-eight-style around two core cords. Where the fibers cross between the core cords, a distinctive, indented line ("the rib") appears on either side of the braid. Also commonly referred to as Russia braid, soutache is one of the basic elements used in passementerie—the French art of textile embellishment encompassing tassel-making, and fringe and clothing decoration such as the swirling braids seen on band and military uniforms. Soutache can be made of many fibers including silk, cotton, acrylic, polyester, rayon, metalized fibers (usually metalized plastic), or any combination thereof and is widely available in $\frac{5}{64}$ inch (2 mm), what is commonly referred to as $\frac{1}{8}$ inch (3 mm, although, in truth, this may range from 2.5 to 3 mm) and $\frac{1}{4}$ inch (6 mm). The $\frac{1}{8}$-inch (3 mm) variety is most commonly used for soutache and embroidery, though I've experimented with other widths and achieved interesting results

These are the most important things to consider when selecting soutache:

Consistency. Finding a product line in which all of the colors are the same width and thickness is the most important characteristic with which to concern yourself. Remember that few brands of soutache were made for jewelry making. Consequently, the manufacturer may or may not be concerned with consistency between colors. In particular, it is important that the width of each braid in a stack be the same size. You may find that—with some manufacturers—one color is a little wider or narrower than the other.

Drape. The relative stiffness or floppiness of a piece of soutache is determined by three things: the tightness of the braiding, the thickness of the core cords, and the fiber content of both the braid's colored, wrapping yarn, and the core cords' penetrability. When soutache is aligned and stacked properly (and assuming your needle is sharp), your needle should pass easily through the stack at the rib. If it is difficult to penetrate the stack, this may be caused by the core cords of the soutache. Soutache with core cords made of plastic or monofilament-type product can be almost impossible to use.

Thread. Use a good-quality nylon beading thread and select a color that coordinates with your design since it will show on the back of the work. I like Nymo brand thread, size B.

Note: For most of the project photographs in this book, I have intentionally selected thread that has a strong contrast to the soutache so that you can see it better in the photographs. For your own projects, however, you may wish to select a thread color that most closely represents the middle value of the colors of soutache you have chosen for your project.

Synthetic suede. Use this fabric for backing. You might also experiment with leather or natural suede.

Figure 1 clearly illustrates how different widths and thicknesses of soutache relate to commonly-used bead sizes. If you want to make big jewelry fast, choose wider soutache and bigger beads. For more delicate creations, select narrower soutache and smaller beads.

Figure 1

Tools

Darning needle. I use a darning needle for adjusting the final shape of a piece after I've glued it down, for poking errant strands of beading wire or thread into place, and even for getting glue exactly where I want it. Because they're made of steel, they can be wiped or scraped clean easily.

Hole punch. A simple office single-hole punch is great for making perfectly round holes in beading foundation and backing material.

Iron. Use a regular household steam iron to bond your fabrics together.

Needles. I use size 10 long beading needles for pretty much everything. If I'm working with size 15° seed beads, I might switch to a size 12.

Pliers. Different types include flat-nose pliers, looping pliers, rosary pliers, and crimping pliers.

Scissors. I recommend having one pair of large, fabric-cutting scissors and a smaller pair of craft or embroidery scissors that has very sharp points designed for cutting into small corners. In addition, a good pair of cuticle or fly-tying scissors can give you great control when cutting away the backing from negative spaces.

Design

Organic versus Planned Design

I am often asked whether I draw out my jewelry designs or I just start working and let whatever happens, happen. I usually just smile and say, "Yes!"

The fact is, soutache and bead embroidery almost begs for the spontaneity of free-form, abstract design (or design that does not depict a person, place, or thing in the natural world).

Some of the happiest hours of my life started with about 20 yards (18.3 m) of soutache, a tray of beads, and not the faintest clue as to where I was headed with any of it. If you are new to soutache and bead embroidery, allowing yourself the opportunity to just create is one of the very best ways to learn. What happens when you turn that stack back on itself? What about when you split a stack asymmetrically? Can you twist that? Fold that? Add a brand new stack right there? If you give yourself permission to work organically, to begin stitching without even knowing

if you're making an earring or a necklace, you can completely focus on the quality of the stitching. And it's OK if you just end up with components. I've made hundreds of pieces of jewelry using little bits and pieces of shmoo that had absolutely no specific destination when they were created and may have even floated around my studio for a few months just looking for something to land on (figure 2).

Figure 2

In my mind, there are levels of planning: there are planned concepts and planned designs.

Planned concepts are concerned with higher-level design aspects: Is this a collar-style necklace? How large should the circumference for the neck hole be? How wide should it be at its widest point? Do I want the design portion of the collar to go all the way around the back of the neck or stop short so that I can attach some adjustable straps? I usually start this kind of planning with a simple computer drawing so that I can print out the images, cut them, and "try on" my paper templates. If I want a larger neck hole or a thinner band, I can easily modify these on the computer screen, reprint, recut, and try again (figures 3 and 4).

Figure 3

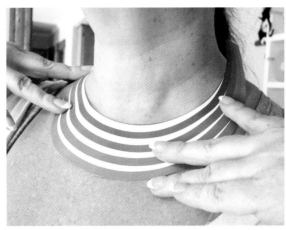

Figure 4

Figure 5

Figure 6

Figure 7

I find that planning my designs is almost always necessary if I'm trying to create a figurative piece (figurative design can be derived from real object sources). Planned design can happen in two ways: It can be a reiteration and refinement of something I've made before (that's the easy way). Or it can be a serious attempt to think through the details of something I really want to make but haven't quite figured out (that's the hard way).

For instance, I got it into my head that I wanted to make a chameleon, so I found a decent photo of a chameleon on the internet, dumped it into my photo-processing software, simplified it, and printed it in different sizes (figure 5). After selecting what I felt would be the most "jewelry" appropriate size, I broke the image down into its basic parts: head, body, and tail. I knew the head was probably going to be the most difficult part but also the part most needed to be recognizably chameleon-like when it was all done. I started working stacks of soutache around beads that already suggested the general shapes I was trying to achieve. I arrived at a decent result, except that the head alone was almost the size of my palm (figure 6). I tried again, aiming for something smaller, and managed to crank out something that was not recognizable as a chameleon's head (figure 7). One more time and I had it. The body and legs went more smoothly but the tail—which I had specifically saved for last because it looked like it would be the most fun—was a disaster! My first attempt yielded a hot mess (figure 8). (Thank goodness for scissors!) But with a little more noodling around, I found a wonderful way to create the tail shape, which needed not only to curve but to increase in size from tip to base (figure 9).

Figure 8

Figure 9

Color

The single biggest thing to take into consideration when thinking about the use of color in soutache and bead embroidery is that no matter what brand of soutache braid you're working with, there will only be so many colors to choose from, and—unlike paint or pastels—the colors cannot truly be physically mixed to create new color. But that does not mean that you cannot create a piece of jewelry that "reads" as whatever color you want using other colors in particular combinations. In fine art, one of the best examples of this is pointillism. Consider the famous Neo-Impressionist painting, "A Sunday Afternoon on the Island of La Grande Jatte" by Georges Seurat. Look carefully at the skirt of the central, female figure. It's pink, right? But zoom in and you see that Seurat used very little actual pink paint to create that shade of pink. Rather, he used individual dabs of cream, rose, tan, lavender, olive, and periwinkle. Our eyes then blend those colors so that we perceive them as being pink.

Figure 10

Figure 11

Let's imagine you want to make a necklace that will be perceived as being coral. Chances are, you're not going to find coral soutache. Pink, mauve, rose, orange, peach—yes, but coral? Probably not. So how do you make a coral-colored necklace? Well you start out by thinking about the color coral. It's a sort of pinky-peach. Or maybe it's a sort of orangey-peachy-pink. . .

Here's a coral colored knit top for which I want to make a matching necklace. I've pulled out a bunch of soutache in colors ranging from pale pink to rust (figure 12).

Figure 12

I began experimenting with different combinations of some of these colors by making lollipops. They all have the same bead, and they all have a four-layer stack, but there are different combinations of colors used in the stack for each lollipop. Comparing them against my knit top, I feel that the one on the far right is the best match (figure 13). There is not one single piece of soutache or one single bead in the piece that is exactly the same color as the knit fabric. But just like Seurat's pointillism, our eyes read the color of the finished work by sort of mushing all the colors together.

Figure 13

CHAPTER 2: **THE BASICS**

When working through any of the projects in Part 3, basic and advanced techniques will be called out in **boldface type**. If you're not sure exactly what to do, just refer back to this chapter for a quick refresher.

Note: As much as is practical, the process photography in this book is designed to keep the viewer oriented with the work and to make sure that the action is clearly visible. To that end, I try to keep my hands out of the pictures. The thing to remember is that while you see the work placed flat on a work surface in the photos, in real life I would be holding the work in my hands and I would turn the work in whatever direction would allow me to stitch toward my nondominant hand. For instance, the instructions for figure 1 would read, "Working from left to right, make one shaping stitch." This is so that you have a clear understanding of where you're going in relation to where you were. But in reality—if you are right-handed—you would probably pick the work up and work from the back as shown in figure 2 so that you could stitch from right to left.

Figure 1

Figure 2

Add a jump ring. Working from the back of the work, sew through the two or three outermost braids so the thread exits the rib where you want your jump ring to be attached (figure 3). Pick up a 6 mm jump ring and make three or four **whipstitches** to secure the jump ring behind the edge of the work (figures 4 and 5).

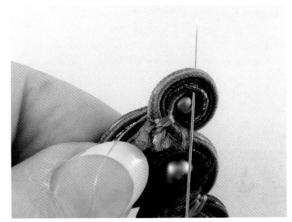
Figure 3

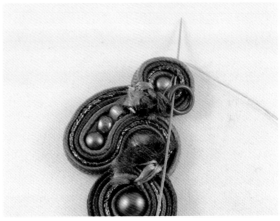
Figure 4

Figure 5

Add a pin backer. Apply a thin line of jewelry glue to the flat side of a pin backer. Use a toothpick to spread it thinly (figure 6) and place pin backer at desired location (figure 7). Allow to dry completely. Fold the synthetic suede in half, right sides together. Lay the fold along the pin backer. Use a pen to mark the hinge and clasp locations on the fold (figure 8). At the marked locations, make a small snip perpendicular to the fold for the hinge (figure 9) and another parallel to the fold for the clasp (figure 10). Fit the synthetic suede over the pin to make sure the snips slip easily over hinge and clasp (figure 11). Put the synthetic suede aside and apply a thin layer of washable fabric glue over the back of the work, avoiding the pin-backer hinge and clasp (figure 12). Replace the synthetic suede—bringing the hinge and clasp through the snips—(figure 13) and allow the glue to dry completely.

Figure 8

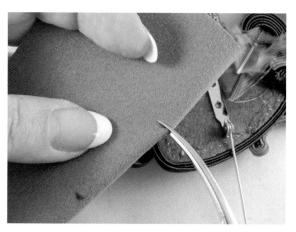

Figure 9

Figure 6

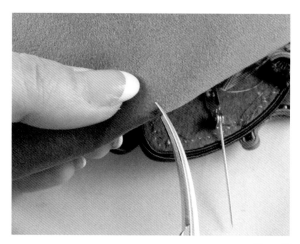

Figure 10

Figure 7

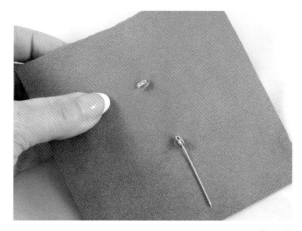

Figure 11

Figure 12

Figure 13

Align and stack. Orient each length of soutache so the weave of the braid is pointed in the same direction as you are looking down on it (figure 14). Stack the soutache braids one on top of the other. Hold the stack from its outer edges to keep the stack aligned (figure 15).

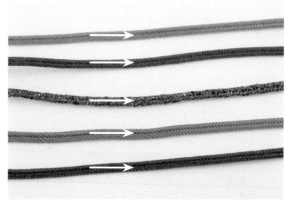

Figure 14

Figure 15

Note: Students often ask if it's important to have all the pieces of soutache aligned and stacked in the same direction. I usually reply that it's a best practice as opposed to a deal breaker. However, properly aligned stacks look better because the direction of those little points corresponds to the diagonal grain of the fibers visible from the front of the finished work (figure 16). When changing a wide curve into a tighter curve, using proper alignment also allows one braid to slide more easily over another, helping to reduce dimples and warps in the curve.

Figure 18

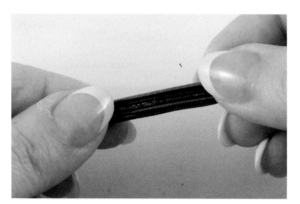

Figure 16

Figure 19

Apply backing. Apply a dab of glue to back of the work (figure 17). Using your finger or a toothpick, spread glue just to the edges of the work (figure 18). Use glue sparingly over the beads so it does not ooze through to the front. The glue should look like a light layer of mayonnaise on a sandwich (figure 19). Place the glued shape on the wrong side of a piece of synthetic suede and let it dry completely (figure 20).

Figure 20

Figure 17

Backstitch 2. One of the basic stitches used in bead embroidery, backstitch 2 is used to lay down a line of beads—often in a curving path. It can be used as a base row to create a peyote-stitch bezel or as an independent, decorative element.

1. Sew up from the bottom of the beading foundation.

2. Pick up two beads (figure 21).

Figure 21

3. Sew down through the beading foundation just barely beyond the end of the second bead (figure 22).

Figure 22

4. Sew back up through the beading foundation so the thread is exiting between the first and second beads (figure 23).

Figure 23

5. Sew through the second bead and pick up two more beads (figure 24).

Figure 24

6. Sew down through the beading foundation just barely beyond the end of the fourth bead.

7. Sew back up through the beading foundation so the thread is exiting between the third and fourth beads (figure 25).

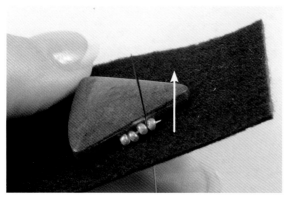

Figure 25

8. Sew through the fourth bead (figure 26) and pick up two more beads.

Figure 26

9. Continue the pattern of sewing through the last bead added and picking up two beads.

Bead chain. Bead chain is made of links created by putting a bead on a head pin and making a **plain loop** on each end. The links are joined to form a chain.

Brick stitch. There are a number of different **edge-beading** techniques, some more decorative than others. Brick stitch is one of the most versatile because the exposed holes of the edge beads allow multiple components to be joined more easily. To work this stitch easily, hold the work so the synthetic suede is facing up.

1. Prepare the thread and **bury the knot**.

2. With thread exiting the rib of the outermost layer of the soutache (figure 27), pick up two 11° seed beads.

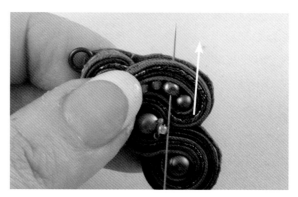

Figure 27

3. Working from left to right, sew through a rib of the soutache (approximately one bead width away from where the thread last exited) and diagonally out the back of synthetic suede very close to edge (figure 28).

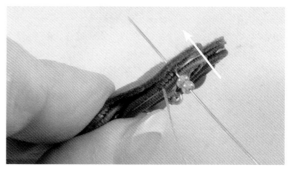

Figure 28

4. Insert needle through the second bead so the thread exits between the first and second bead (figure 29).

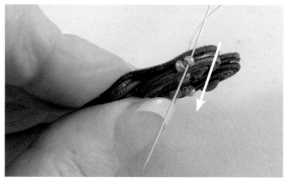

Figure 29

5. Pick up another 11° seed bead and sew through the rib of the soutache (approximately half a bead width away from the last bead) and out the back of the synthetic suede very close to edge (figure 30).

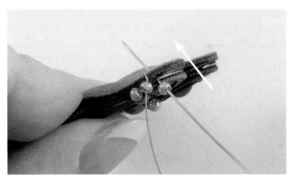

Figure 30

6. Insert needle through the last bead, exiting between last and second-to-last beads (figure 31).

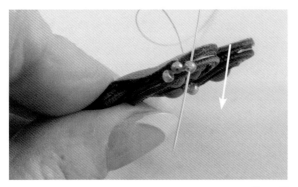

Figure 31

7. Repeat steps 5 and 6 until you've gone all the way around. After you've added five or six beads, you will begin to see the beads "stand up" with their holes facing outward (figure 32).

Figure 32

8. When you reach the first 11° seed bead added in step 2, sew through it, entering the hole between the first and second bead (figure 33) and passing through the soutache and the synthetic suede. Sew back up through the first bead. Sew down through the second bead, through the soutache and synthetic suede (figure 34).

Figure 33

Figure 34

9. Bury the thread.

Bury the knot. Prepare the thread. From the front of the work, sew through one of the larger beads and through the soutache (figure 35) so the thread is exiting at the desired location. The knot will be buried inside the bead or between the bead and the inner strand of soutache.

Figure 35

Bury the thread. Slide the needle underneath three or four of the blanket stitches created by the edge beading and trim the thread (figures 36 and 37). You don't need to knot the thread.

Figure 36   Figure 37

Centered loop. Use flat-nose pliers to make a 90° bend approximately ⅜ inch (9.5 mm) away from the end of a head pin (figure 38). While firmly holding the base of head pin with the flat-nose pliers, use 6-in-1, rosary, round-nose, or bail-forming pliers to turn the end of head pin into a loop (figure 39).

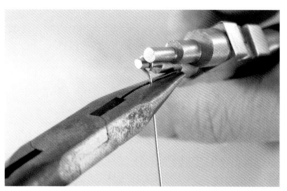

Figure 38

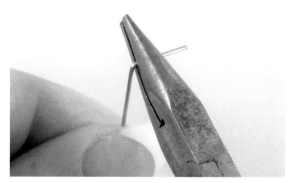

Figure 39

Consolidate stack. In preparation for **ending a stack**, use **shaping stitches** to sew all of the strands of braid in a stack together so that when the stack is curved behind the work the strands do not spread apart.

Couching. This is a technique used to embellish an area of bead embroidery. Sew up through the beading foundation right next to where two beads meet (figure 40). Pick up a run of smaller beads (the size and number of beads will vary based on the design, but they are most often 11° or 15° seed beads) (figure 41). Sew down over first row of beads (figure 42).

Figure 40

Figure 41

Figure 42

Create a bridge. Bridges are built over joins and are usually comprised of a series of three beads. They are decorative additions to the work and are useful in hiding a join that did not close up as tightly as you might like.

1. Adjacent to any join, sew from the back of the work to the front of the work so the thread is exiting the innermost braid, above the bead but below the join (figure 43).

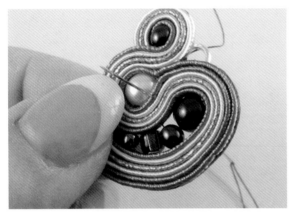

Figure 43

2. Pick up one small bead, one slightly larger bead, and another small bead. (This may mean an 11°, 8°, and 11° seed bead or a 15°, 11°, and 15° seed bead, depending on the scale of the work.) (figure 44).

Figure 44

3. Stitch down through the front of work at the corresponding point on the opposite side of the join (figure 45).

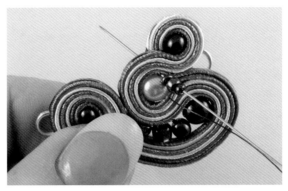

Figure 45

4. Sew back up through the work so the thread is exiting the innermost braid near and slightly below the join (figure 46).

Figure 46

5. Sew through the middle bead (figure 47).

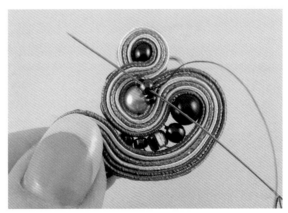

Figure 47

6. Stitch down through the front of work at the corresponding point on the opposite side of the join (figure 48). This second stitch secures the bridge to the work and creates a slight curve (figure 49).

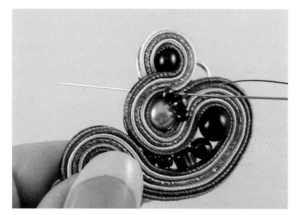

Figure 48

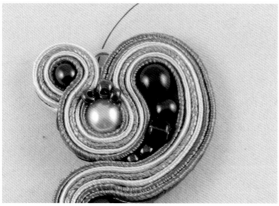

Figure 49

End the stack. Pull the stack behind the work, holding the work between your thumb and forefinger (figure 50). Secure the intersection with three pairs of **tacking stitches** (figure 51). Turn the work over and **whipstitch** through all the braids in the working stack. When sewing through the stack, the thread goes through the rib (figure 52). Repeat five or six times, keeping the stitches in the same location until a smooth girdle of thread builds up (figure 53). There is no need to increase the thread tension. Trim the ends of the braid (figure 54).

Figure 50

Figure 51

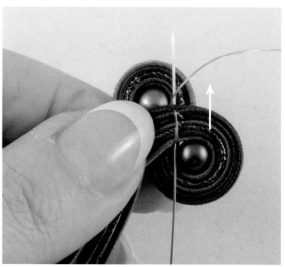

Figure 52

Figure 53

Figure 54

Note: The mnemonic device for remembering how to end a stack is "wrap, tack, whip, and snip."

Ladders. A **ladder** is any succession of beads stitched between two separated stacks; each stitch connecting the two stacks holds one bead. These connections become the "rungs" of the ladder. Ladders can be straight or curved, graduated or even, closed or open, secured or independent. (For more information on these variations, see Additional Techniques, Ladders.)

1. From outside of any stack pair, sew through one stack (figure 55).

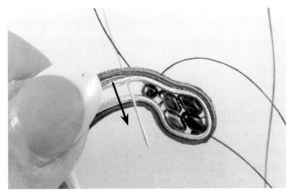

Figure 55

2. Pick up a bead and sew through the second stack from the inside to outside (figure 56).

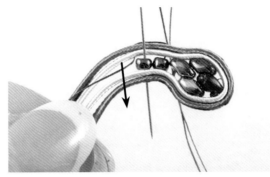

Figure 56

3. Make one shaping stitch so the thread exits the stack approximately one bead width away from where it entered (figure 57).

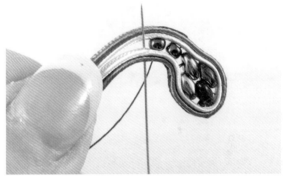

Figure 57

4. Pick up another bead. Sew through the first stack from the inside to the outside (figure 58).

Figure 58

5. Repeat steps 1 through 4 as needed.

One-sided join. To create a clean join around a bead that is connected to a secured stack, the innermost braid must be joined first.

1. Pick up a bead and sew through the stack where the hole of the bead will meet the stack (figure 59).

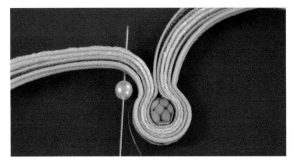

Figure 59

2. Take one long shaping stitch so the thread exits the bottom of the working stack just beyond the bead. Sew through the secured stack very close to the bead (figure 60).

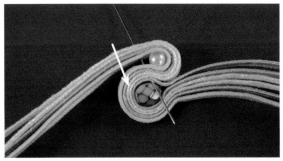

Figure 60

3. Sew back through the secured stack and the innermost strand of the working stack only (figure 61).

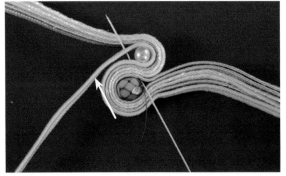

Figure 61

4. Sew back down through the innermost strand and into the secured stack (figure 62).

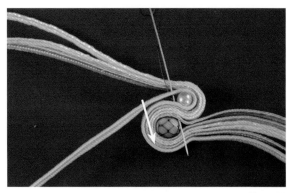

Figure 62

5. Sew back up through the secured stack and the entire working stack (figure 63).

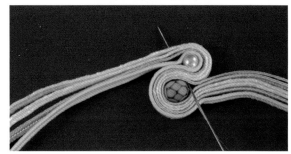

Figure 63

6. Sew back down through the working stack and into the secured stack (figure 64).

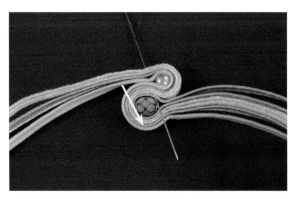

Figure 64

7. Sew up through both the secured and working stacks so the thread is exiting the join to continue on with the work (figure 65).

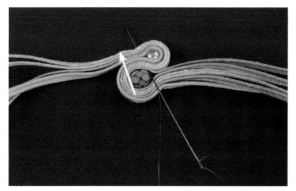

Figure 65

Prepare the thread. Cut a 36-inch (91.4 cm) length of thread. Pull approximately 9 inches (22.9 cm) of thread through the eye of a needle (figure 66). Tie two overhand knots on the other end of the thread (figure 67). Trim the tail close to the knots (figure 68).

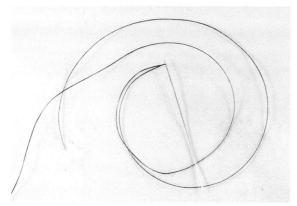

Figure 66

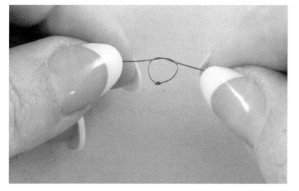

Figure 67

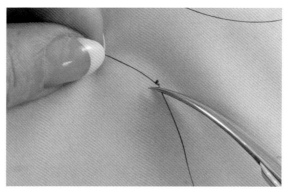

Figure 68

Alternatively, you can make a quilter's knot. This takes some practice but is ultimately a real time-saver. Using your dominant hand, pinch the tail of the thread to the needle so the tail is pointed toward the eye (figure 69). Use your nondominant hand to wrap the thread six or seven times around the needle (figure 70).

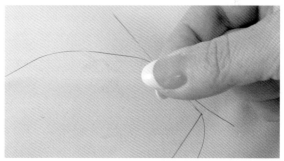

Figure 69

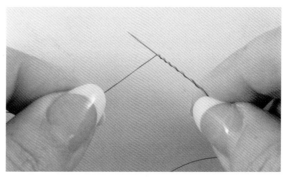

Figure 70

Firmly pinch the coiled thread and the needle between the thumb and forefinger of your nondominant hand (figure 71). Use your dominant hand to pull the needle through coil, keeping a firm grip on the coil with your nondominant hand (figure 72 and 73). A nice, fat knot should appear near the tail of your thread. Trim the tail of the knot (figure 74).

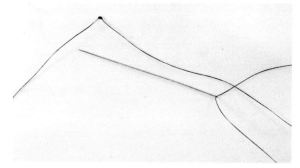

Note: If you are not getting a knot when trying to make a quilter's knot, you are probably starting out by making a U shape (tail to point of needle) instead of an O shape (tail to eye of needle).

Secured stacks. Secured stacks have been connected to the work, and their shape is final. The stack that wraps the central bead of a lollipop, for example, has been secured. The loose, unstitched lengths of braid hanging below the **lollipop** can still be sculpted into any shape or form; they are considered working stacks (figure 75).

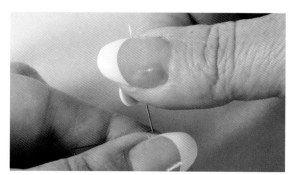

Figure 72

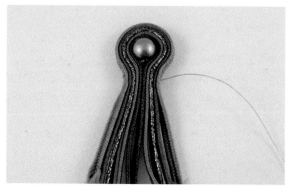

Figure 75

Set the stitch. Retrace a thread path two or three times at a particular location to prepare for turning the stack in such a way that it might put strain on the work, causing thread to show. Setting a stitch does not require an increase in thread tension; simply retracing will lock the work at that spot.

Shallow stitches. When working on beading foundation, you can end your thread by taking two or three shallow stitches in the back of the work: simply slide your needle under the surface of the beading foundation without letting the needle escape to the front of the work (figure 76). Repeat once or twice. There is no need to make a knot.

Figure 71

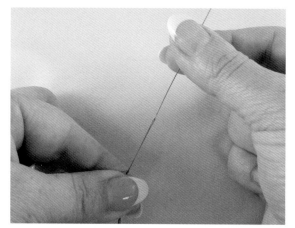

Figure 73

Figure 76

Shaping stitches. Shaping stitches serve two functions: to consolidate a stack—meaning to hold all of the braids together so that the stack can be handled as a single element—and to hold the curve into which the stack has been sculpted. There are two variations of shaping stitches—standard and invisible.

The standard shaping stitch is really just a variation on the running stitch (simply sewing up and down repeatedly while moving continuously in one direction). These should be longer on the outside of the curve—about ¼ to ⅜ inch (6 to 9.5 mm) and shorter inside the curve—about 1/16 inch (1.6 mm). Shaping stitches are always taken through the ribs of the soutache, meaning that the needle is driven up through the stack where the fibers of each braid come together in a V. The stack should be held in alignment so the needle passes through all the ribs in the stack. When done correctly, the outside stitches will nestle into the rib and—assuming you are working with an appropriate thread color—will be unobtrusive. In most cases, these stitches will be covered either by more work being built on top of them or by edge beading.

1. Holding the stack in the desired curve and working from right to left, sew down through the stack about a ¼ inch (6 mm) to the left (figure 77). (This counts as *one* shaping stitch.)

2. Sew up through the stack about 1/16 inch (1.6 mm) to the left (figure 78). (This counts as the second shaping stitch).

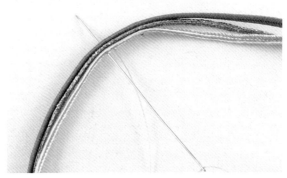

Figure 78

Repeat steps 1 and 2 as needed with the understanding that a shaping stitch is one stitch, irrespective of length or whether it is inside or outside of the curve.

Invisible shaping stitches are used in areas where **standard shaping stitches** might be too conspicuous, such as independent ladders or sections that are not going to be edge beaded. Similar to standard shaping stitches, invisible shaping stitches consolidate stacks and hold their curves. The needle is inserted diagonally through the stack each time, however, resulting in the smallest possible stitch showing on either side of the stack. These stitches are a little harder to master, but they are well worth the effort.

1. Holding the stack in the desired curve and working from right to left, sew down through the stack diagonally as close as possible to where the thread last exited (figure 79).

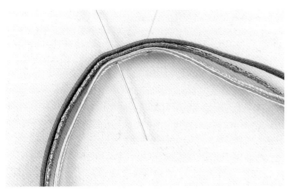

Figure 77

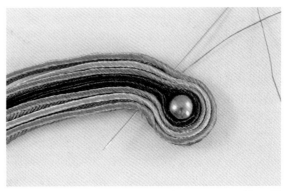

Figure 79

2. Sew up through the stack diagonally as close as possible to where the thread last exited (figure 80).

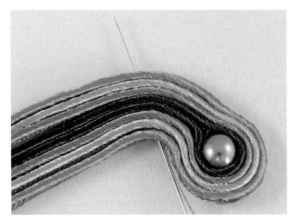

Figure 80

Repeat steps 1 and 2 as needed.

Step up. In this book, **peyote stitch** is often used to create bezels to secure cabochons. Peyote stitch is created by weaving circular rows of beads one on top of another. After completing a row, "stepping up" means sewing through the first bead in the row and then adding a new bead which will become the first bead in the next row up.

Tacking stitches. Tacking stitches are always completed in two movements: the first, back to front, and the second, front to back. In soutache and bead embroidery, tacking stitches are most commonly used while **ending stacks** to secure the **working stack** behind the **secured stack**. They are also used to attach one component to another. Tacking stitches are almost never made in the rib. Rather, threads of tacking stitches are likely to enter and exit either between individual pieces of soutache or even directly through the side of a piece of soutache. It is important when making the front-to-back portion of the tacking stitch to sew down as closely as possible to where the thread last exited. The fibers of the soutache will open up and essentially "absorb" the stitch so that it is not visible on the front of the work.

1. Sew up from back of the work (figure 81).

Figure 81

2. Sew back down through all the layers, inserting the needle as closely as possible to the point where the thread exited (figure 82).

Figure 82

Trace a path. Sometimes it is desirable to get from one area of the work to another without pulling the thread across the back or cutting and reknotting it. Simply sew through the front of the work. Keep the stitches inconspicuous by burying them in the soutache stacks or going through the holes of larger beads until the thread is exiting the desired location.

Train. While most of the process photos in this book are shown with the work lying flat on a surface, in truth, you will usually hold the work in both hands. Training refers to the practice of repeatedly stroking and curving the loose strands of the working stack into the desired curve as you use the shaping stitches to gently secure them into place.

Trim the backing. After the glue has dried completely, trim away the excess synthetic suede. Be sure to trim synthetic suede from behind exposed portions of jump rings (figure 83). Do not to overtrim; soutache should *not* be visible from the back of the work. A thin outline of synthetic suede should be visible from the front of the work (figure 84).

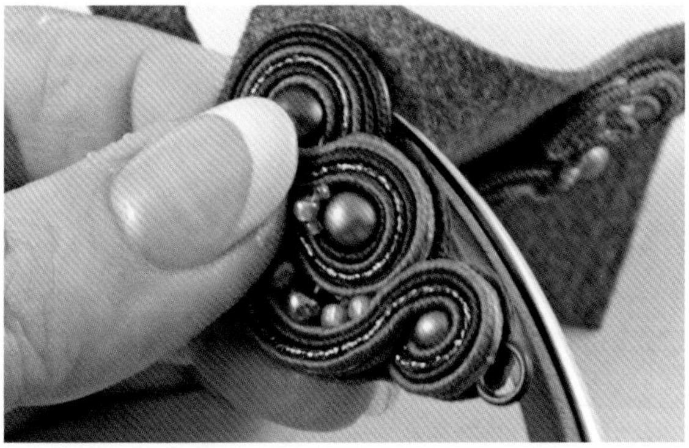

Figure 83

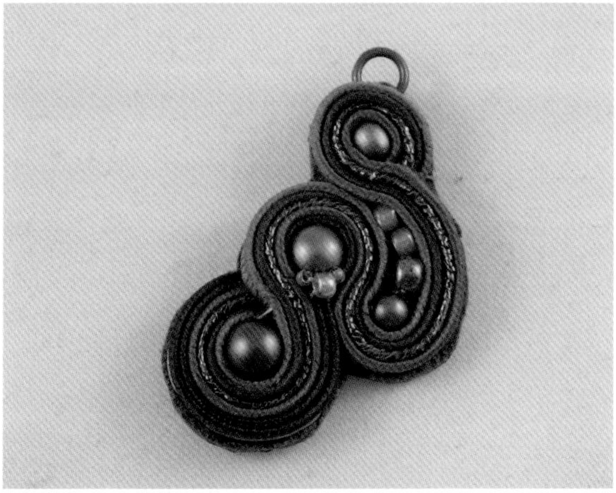

Figure 84

Trim the foundation. After the bead embroidery has been completed, trim away the excess beading foundation (figure 85). Do not overtrim; bead embroidery should *not* be visible from back of work. Keep your cutting as smooth and even as possible. Be careful not to trim stitches. A thin outline of beading foundation should be visible from front of work.

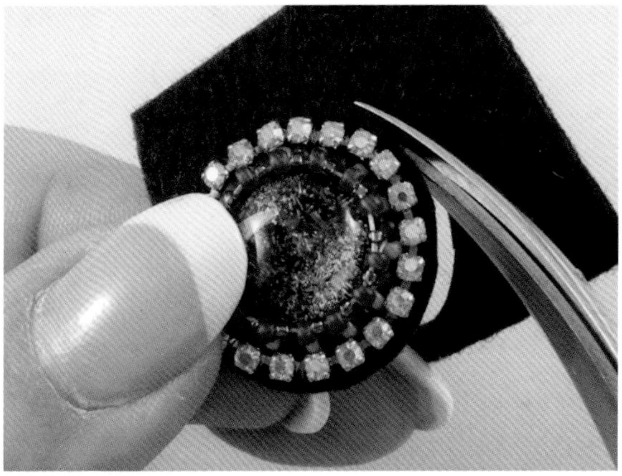

Figure 85

Two-sided join. To create a clean join around a round bead or at any area of a bead that causes the stacks to come together at an obtuse angle, the two innermost braids must be joined first.

1. Separate the stacks of braids and pinch together the innermost braids of both stacks under the bead or element that has been wrapped (figure 86). The thread should be coming toward you, not out the back of the work.

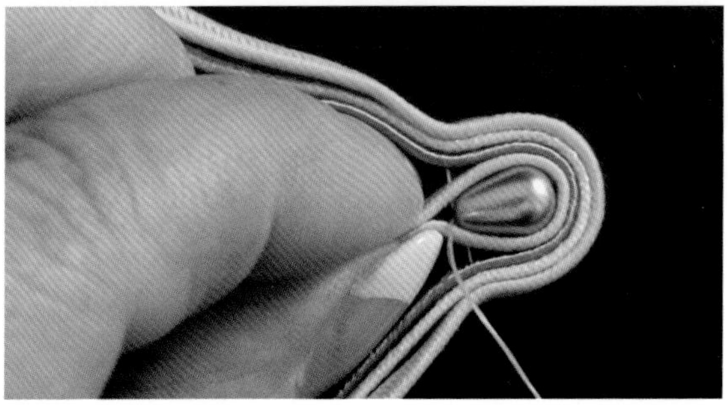

Figure 86

2. Sew through the upper, innermost braid only from inside to outside (figure 87).

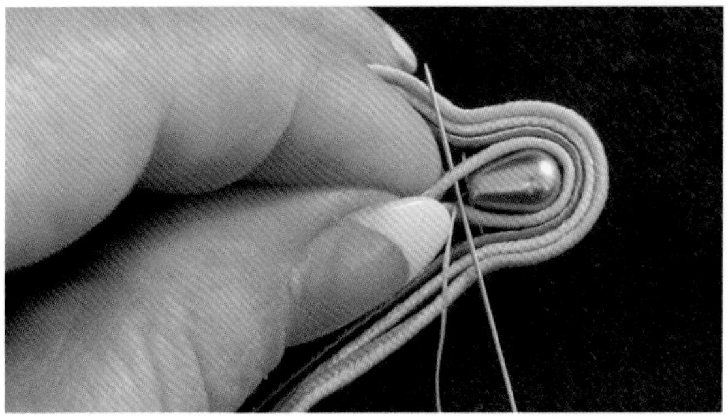

Figure 87

3. Sew down through both innermost braids (figure 88).

Figure 88

4. Sew up through both innermost braids and all the remaining braids in the upper stack (figure 89).

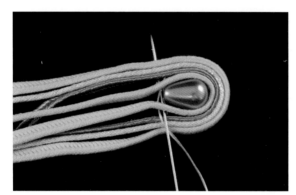

Figure 89

5. Sew down through entire large stack (figure 90). Note that no additional thread tension has been added up to this point.

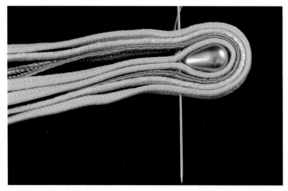

Figure 90

6. Keeping the thread close to the bead, retrace the thread path two or three times, slightly increasing thread tension with each successive pass until the join looks clean (figure 91).

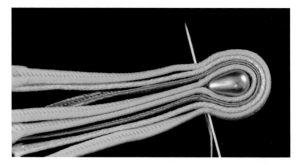

Figure 91

When making joins, keep your stitches very close to the bead being wrapped—do not travel down the "stick" of the **lollipop.** You will sew over previous stitches, and that is OK.

Whipstitches. Whipstitches are used most frequently for **ending stacks** and adding jump rings. Sew through the work at the desired location, pushing the needle away from you. Pull the needle and thread back toward yourself and sew through the work again at the exact same location (figure 92). Repeat as necessary.

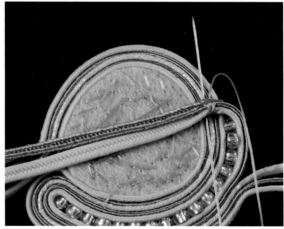

Figure 92

Working stack. As you stitch stacks in place, they become **"secured stacks"** meaning that they can no longer change shape. The remaining loose or floppy strands whose final shape and placement have yet to be determined are referred to as "working stacks."

Tips & Tricks

One of the most common things I hear students say when I'm teaching classes (besides, "Holy cow! I udderly *love* this stuff!") is "Wow . . . I don't think I would have been able to figure that out on my own." This usually relates to some pointer I've given that I think of as a tip or a trick. But it is really nothing more than a solution I've devised to overcome a problem I've encountered or some silly mistake I've made about—oh—five gazillion times. In this chapter, I have endeavored to gather the bulk of this life-changing wisdom.

Aligning and stacking with the canapé method. Sometimes the first challenge is simply being able get a good grip on the materials. Typically, I use the "bird's beak method"—simply orienting each braid one at a time and placing them between the thumb and forefinger of my nondominant hand. My thumb and forefinger are pinched to form a "bird's beak," and the soutache is simply draped in the V (figure 93). Some folks have trouble with this, however, and will try to grip or roll the soutache.

Figure 93

Bead spacing. Beads don't bend. When creating a **ladder**, crowding the beads will result in "ruffling" (one bead moving toward the back of the work, one toward the front, one toward the back, and so on) (figure 94).

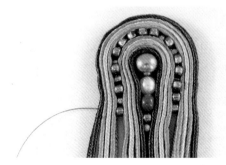

Figure 94

Cut generously. A common mistake made by those new to soutache and bead embroidery is to be a little too frugal with the soutache. No matter what you do, those ends are going to fray, so don't get in the habit of continuously trimming them. When designing your own work, cut your lengths a little longer than you think you need (all of the instructions in this book allow for extra length, so you don't need to add more to *those* measurements). This will eliminate the frustration of fiddling with frays when **ending stacks**.

Making smooth curves. What first drew me to the art of soutache and bead embroidery was the seemingly complex interplay of elegant curvilinear shapes undulating over and around one another. The smoothness of those curves, however, can be elusive when first working with soutache. Here are three tricks for achieving smooth organic lines.

Don't stitch it straight. Because aligning and stacking can feel a bit foreign the first few times, it's common for students to get the idea that the best thing to do is to line the braids up on their bead mat, consolidate the stack in a nice straight line so they can control it, and then bend it into a curve (figure 95). This will never work. The basic geometry at work here is that of concentric circles. The curve on the outside has a greater circumference than the one on the inside. Stitching the soutache together in a straight line means consolidating braids of equal length so the one that's supposed to be on the outside is too short and the one on the inside is too long. This causes warps, kinks, and breaks in the line. You must stitch into the curve (figure 96). Gravity will do most of the work for you—just hold the work so the stacks hang down left and right of where you're holding it and—shazam!—you've got a curve.

Figure 95

Figure 96

Note: It is important to note that the stitches do not curve the stack. Your fingers sculpt the stack into (or close to) the curve you want, and stitches hold that form in place.

Stitch it where you hold it. When you've created a stack, the only place it is perfectly aligned is where you are holding it between your thumb and forefinger. Stitching into the stack even ½ inch (1.3 cm) away can result in the needle not going through the rib of each braid but slipping toward the front or back of one piece or another (figure 97). Get in the habit of running the needle through the stack directly between your thumb and forefinger (figure 98). In the beginning, this is difficult because you want to keep looking under the stack to see if the needle is in the rib. Believe me, if you are holding the stack correctly, the needle will go through the rib simply because it offers the path of least resistance.

Figure 97

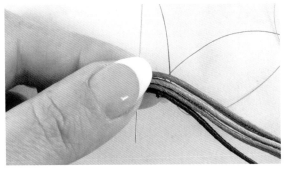

Figure 98

Note: Stitching up or down between your thumb and forefinger means you are always stitching toward your nondominant hand. The photographs in this book are always oriented the same way. If I'm showing you the work from the front, I will most likely continue to show you the work from the front. This means that sometimes it looks like I'm working from right to left and sometimes left to right. In reality, however, I flip my work back and forth as I work so that I am always working from right to left because I am right-handed. You should flip your work from front to back so that you are always pushing the needle toward your nondominant hand.

Zero thread tension. Long-time bead weavers always gasp when I say this as they have been trained to put tremendous tension into their work. But bead weaving and soutache and bead embroidery use two entirely different skill sets. In soutache and bead embroidery, putting too much tension on your thread can result in dimples on the outer edge of your work (soutache cellulite!) (figure 99) and "locking" (when one layer of soutache seems to disappear from a stack because it has been pulled to the back of the work) (figure 100). When pulling your thread through your stack, here are two important things to keep in the back of your mind:

Figure 99

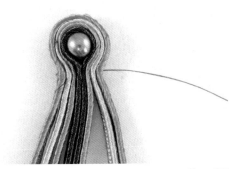

Figure 100

Aspire to the bubble. As you are pulling your thread down through the stack, pull only until you can still imagine that a breath of air could pass underneath the line of thread you have created on top of the stack (figure 101).

Figure 101

Eyes on the line. When the jewelry is backed and finished, what your eye will perceive are the lines of the stacks. When we're working, however, it is tempting to focus too much on the connection between the beads and stack. Most of the time, each bead will "kiss" the stack on both sides, but beads do not come in an infinite array of sizes, and beads can be inconsistent. This means that a bead may be too small to touch the stack on both sides. It's natural in this case to want to pull the thread until the stack conforms to the bead, but this will resull in breaking the natural, smooth curve of the stack. This will be very obvious when the work is finished (figure 102).

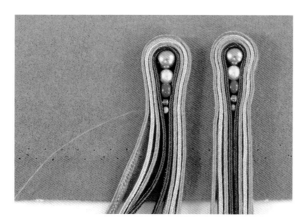

Figure 102

Mirrors. Making mirrored shapes does not have to be confusing, and you don't need to work "backward" if you follow this technique. To mirror an existing shape, make the shape exactly like it right up until the point that you need to end the stack (figure 103). Now, if I were to end the stack behind the work (figure 104), I'd be well on my way to creating a duplicate instead of a mirror. But, if I pull the stack on top of the work (figure 105) and then flip the work over (figure 106), you can see that a mirror image has already begun to form. End the stack this way and then carry on with the work; once you've ended a stack, the front and back are very obvious, so it's hard to mess it up (figure 107).

Figure 103

Figure 104

Figure 105

Figure 106

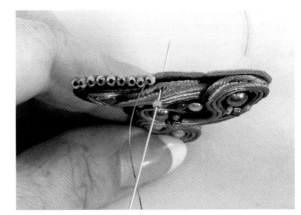

Figure 109

Figure 107

Figure 110

Plane changes. When **edge beading**, there's always a point where one stack crosses behind another, and jumping from one level to the other can look and feel awkward. To make the transition smoother, attach one edge bead to the backing material only before moving up or down to the next stack (figures 108, 109, and 110).

Surface diving. Some projects require sewing through very tall stacks made up of many layers of braid. Remember that soutache is very forgiving—it is not imperative that every single stitch goes through the stack in one fell swoop. It's OK to sew partially through a stack, come up for air either in the front or the back, and then dive back down to get out the other side (figures 111 and 112).

Figure 108

Figure 111

Figure 112

Figure 114

Wrapping and gluing frays. Once you learn how to **end a stack** properly, glue shouldn't be used to bring your stacks to the back. We have all been in the position, however, of cutting our soutache a smidgeon shorter than we really needed. Sometimes that's simply a matter of misjudgment, and other times it's the result of trying to be overly frugal. But the result is the same: trying to wrestle a fuzzy, frayed end onto the back of the work (figure 113). If you can see that one of your braids is going to be too short, dab a little glue on it and let it dry before proceeding. If you're ending the stack and the frays are rebelling, add a few extra **whipstitches** to lock them down and then dab on a little glue (figure 114). Remember that half of the depth of the work is going to be covered by **edge beading**, so even if things look like they're unraveling toward the rear edge of the work, chances are they're not going to show (figure 115).

Figure 115

Figure 113

CHAPTER 3: **ADDITIONAL TECHNIQUES**

Handling Stacks

Stacks

The core material used in soutache and bead embroidery is, of course, soutache, and any group of strands, one laid on top of another, flat to flat, is referred to as a "stack." Stacks may diverge (split), converge (join), or cross. Many components—and even whole projects—begin with a single stack that joins and splits repeatedly with no additional stacks being added. When creating soutache jewelry, it is important to understand the "anatomy" of the work. Figure 1 shows a single stack made of six strands of soutache wrapped around a marquise-shaped bead to form a lollipop (figure 1). The part of the stack that actually wraps the bead is referred to as the "secured stack," as its form can no longer be altered. The twelve loose strands of braid sticking out below the join is the "working stack"—its final form has myriad possibilities yet to be determined. Note that all twelve strands are currently considered the "stack." Even though it is very large—until it is split—it is considered to be one thing.

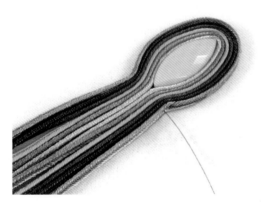

Figure 1

The lollipop is a basic shape. It is an unfinished shape since it still has a working stack and cannot be effectively backed and finished, but it is core to many projects and designs.

Making a Lollipop

1. Cut four 8-inch (20.3 cm) lengths of soutache.

2. Prepare the thread and **align and stack** the cut lengths. Locate the center of the stack and sew up through the stack at the rib (figure 2).

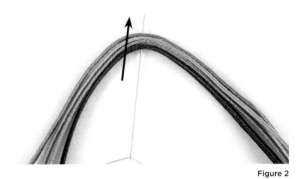

Figure 2

3. Working from right to left, make three* **shaping stitches** (figure 3).

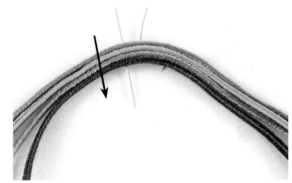

Figure 3

4. Pick up a 6 mm bead and sew up through the stack close to the knot (you can sew either to the left or the right of the knot—just don't try to sew through the knot) (figure 4).

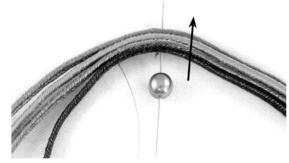

Figure 4

5. Working from left to right, make three* shaping stitches (figure 5).

Figure 5

6. Entering the bead hole *farthest away* from where the thread is currently exiting, sew up through the bead and stack (figure 6).

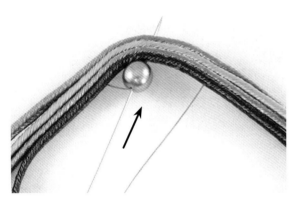

Figure 6

7. Sew back down through the stack and bead (figure 7).

Figure 7

8. Create a **two-sided join** under the bead (figure 8).

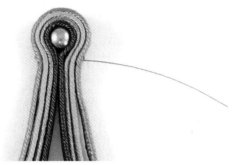

Figure 8

Note: These instructions are specifically for making a lollipop around a 6 mm bead. If you are working with a different size or shape of bead, you may need to change the number of shaping stitches (always keeping an odd number* of stitches on each side of the bead) or the length of the outside shaping stitches.

This bead has been surrounded by two stacks (figure 9). There are two joins—one at each end of the bead. Whether you look at this piece as one large stack that was split before the bead was added or two stacks that were joined before the bead was added, the end result is that there are two separate secured stacks surrounding the bead as opposed to one continuous one as in a lollipop.

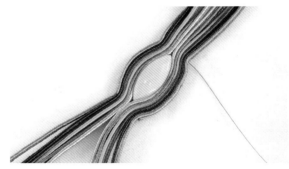

Figure 9

Working with secondary stacks involves attaching a new stack to work already in progress. **Ladders** are a common way to do this, but you can also add soutache directly to a secured stack (figure 10) using **shaping stitches**. Note that the needle exits the back of the work, and it is not critical to go through the entire secured stack—the first two or three layers will suffice (figure 11).

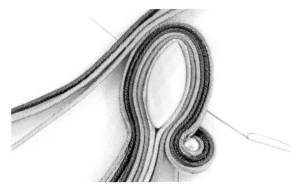

Figure 10

Figure 11

Joins

Joins happen when two stacks converge. The two most common methods, **one-sided joins** and **two-sided joins**, are discussed in chapter 2. The simplest type of join—simply sewing one stack to another—is used in adding secondary stacks and is described in **Stacks**. It's important to know, however, that stacks can also be crossed. This technique is particularly effective in making work that is reminiscent of Celtic knots.

Crossing Stacks

1. To practice crossing stacks, work steps 1 through 5 of **Making a Lollipop** (figure 12).

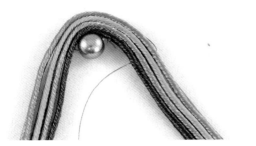

Figure 12

2. Pull the right stack over the left and hold them between the thumb and forefinger of your nondominant hand (figure 13).

Figure 13

3. Sew down on a diagonal so the thread enters the top (previously "right") stack at the rib and exits the bottom (previously "left") stack at the rib (figure 14).

Figure 14

4. Retrace the thread path through the bottom and top stacks (figure 15).

Figure 15

5. On the top (now "left") stack and working from the top down, make three **shaping stitches** (figure 16).

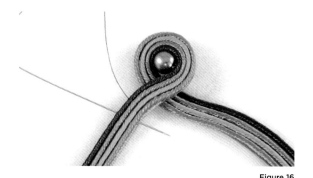

Figure 16

6. Pick up a 6 mm bead. Sew up through the bottom (now "right") stack (figure 17).

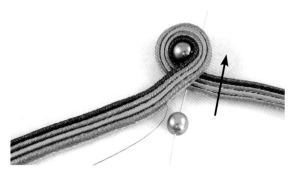

Figure 17

7. Working from the top down, make three shaping stitches (figure 18).

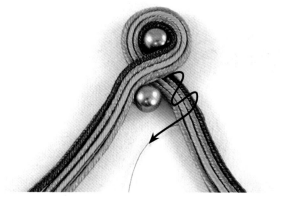

Figure 18

8. Repeat steps 2 through 7 for as many beads as you would like to incorporate into your work (figure 19)

Figure 19

Splits

A stack can split at any point. It often happens after a join, where two stacks have come together, but any working stack can be split at any point. A split in which the stack is divided equally is a **symmetrical split** (figure 20). A split in which the stack is divided unequally is an **asymmetrical split** (figure 21). The number of splits possible is determined only by the number of soutache strands in the stack. It is recommended that stacks be at least two braids thick (figure 22).

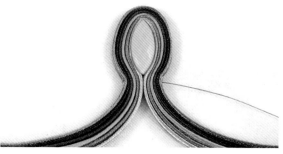

Figure 20

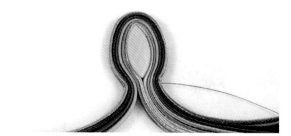

Figure 21

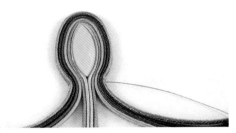

Figure 22

The lasagna stitch is made by splitting a large stack into three or more smaller stacks and adding a bead at each split. The strands of the working stacks are then redistributed, creating new splits and adding a bead at each of those.

Lasagna Stitch

1. Begin with a 12-strand stack. Stacks made in multiples of six work well for this, but feel free to experiment! Try different stack sizes, numbers of stacks, and bead sizes (figure 23).

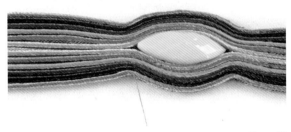

Figure 23

2. With thread exiting the bottom of the stack, separate the large stack into four—a two-strand, two four-strands, and a two-strand (figure 24).

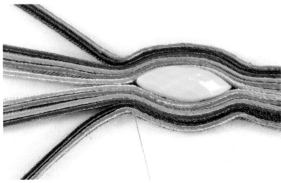

Figure 24

3. Sew up through the bottom stack so the thread exits very close to the split (figure 25).

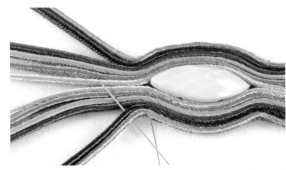

Figure 25

4. Pick up an 8° seed bead. Sew up through the next stack (figure 26).

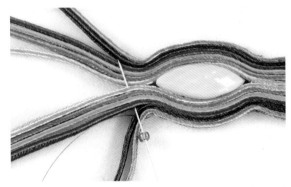

Figure 26

5. Work as in steps 3 and 4, adding an 8° seed bead at each of the next two splits (figure 27).

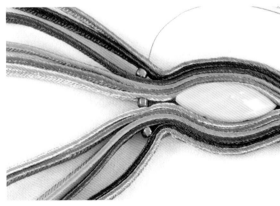

Figure 27

6. Retrace the thread path through all four stacks and three beads (figure 28).

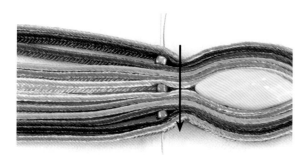

Figure 28

7. Redistribute the stacks: Split the two four-strand stacks symmetrically. Sew up through the bottom four strands of soutache, effectively creating a new join (figure 29).

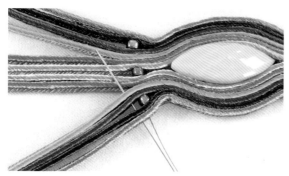

Figure 29

8. Pick up an 8° seed bead and sew up through the next four strands (figure 30).

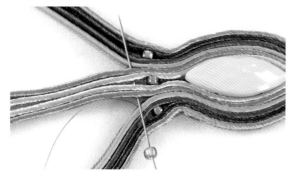

Figure 30

9. Repeat step 8.

10. Retrace the thread path through all three stacks and two beads (figure 31).

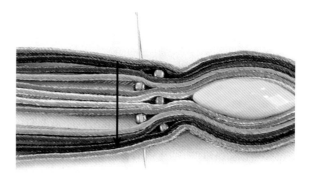

Figure 31

11. Redistribute the stacks as in step 2 (figure 32).

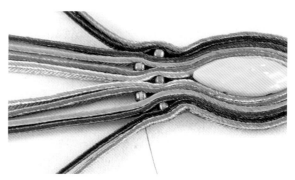

Figure 32

12. Continue working as in steps 3 through 11 as desired (figure 33).

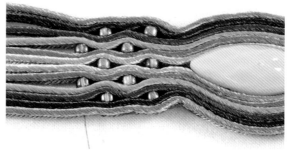

Figure 33

Spirals

Spirals are great—they can be treated like beads, used as a foundation for other work, layered over other things, or grouped together to make all kinds of fun, polka-dot projects. I've included spirals in this chapter because—technically—they're stacks, each layer of soutache laid flat to the one before it. It's just that they're also all the same *piece*.

Simple Spiral

1. Cut an 8-inch (20.3 cm) length of soutache (if you want your spiral to be bigger or smaller, cut a longer or shorter piece accordingly).

2. Prepare the thread. Sew up through the soutache approximately 1 inch (2.5 cm) from the right end (figure 34).

Figure 34

3. Fold the soutache over the knot. The fold is at a 45° angle so the two legs are at a 90° angle (figure 35).

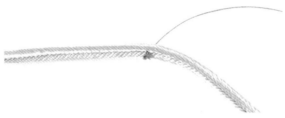

Figure 35

4. Sew through the fold very close to the knot (figure 36).

Figure 36

5. Twist the 1 inch (2.5 cm) stem 180° clockwise so the long end of the soutache wraps behind the fold. Sew through the fold and the new layer of soutache (figure 37).

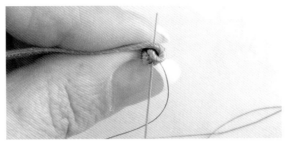

Figure 37

6. Repeat step 5 several times until the spiral is about ⅜ inch (9.5 mm) in diameter (figure 38).

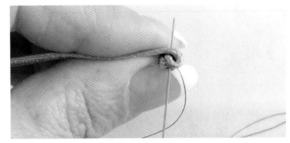

Figure 38

7. Turn the work over.

8. Working from the back, turn the work counterclockwise one quarter turn. Sew into the work at the rib on a slight diagonal so the thread exits the back of the work (figure 39).

Figure 39

9. Repeat step 8 until the spiral is the desired size. When working from the back, this stitching method will result in long, diagonal stitches circling the back of the work (figure 40).

Figure 40

10. Trim off the stem close to the work (figure 41).

Figure 41

11. Fold the remaining soutache to the back of the work and use **tacking stitches** to secure it in place (figure 42). Trim off any excess length (figure 43).

Figure 42

Figure 43

Bicolored Spiral

1. Cut two 8-in (20.3 cm) lengths of soutache.

2. Prepare the thread. Align and stack the soutache.

3. Work as for a **Simple Spiral** (figure 44) until the spiral is the desired size.

Figure 44

4. End the braids on opposite sides of the spiral to keep it as round as possible.

Spiral around a Bead

1. Cut an 8-inch (20.3 cm) length of soutache (if you want your spiral to be bigger or smaller, cut a longer or shorter piece).

2. Prepare the thread. Sew up through the soutache approximately 1½ inches (3.8 cm) from the right end (figure 45).

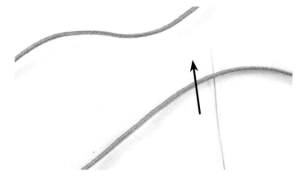

Figure 45

3. Working from left to right, make one **shaping stitch** (figure 46).

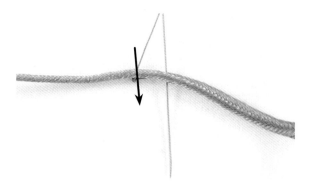

Figure 46

4. Pick up a 4 mm bead and sew up through the soutache close to the knot (figure 47).

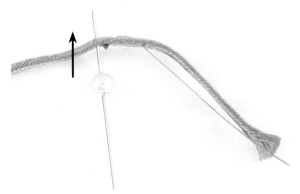

Figure 47

5. Snug the bead into the soutache and wrap the long end over the short end. Sew through the soutache, bead, and double layer of soutache on other side of the bead (figure 48).

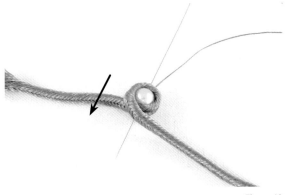

Figure 48

6. Turn the bead clockwise one half turn, wrapping the long end farther around the bead. Sew through all the layers (figure 49).

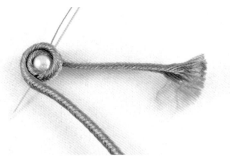

Figure 49

7. Continue working as in step 6 until the spiral is about the size of a dime. Work as for **Simple Spiral**.

Fast Spiral

1. Cut an 8-in (20.3 cm) length of soutache (if you want your spiral to be bigger or smaller, cut a longer or shorter piece).

2. Prepare the thread. Sew up through the soutache at the center (figure 50).

Figure 50

3. Fold the soutache over the knot (figure 51).

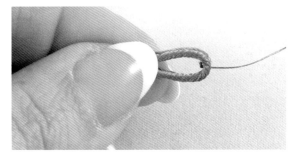

Figure 51

4. Sew up through both layers very close to fold (figure 52).

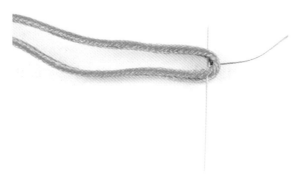

Figure 52

5. Retrace the thread path through both layers.

6. Working from right to left, make a small **invisible shaping stitch**. Pull the thread taut, causing the folded end to curve down (figure 53).

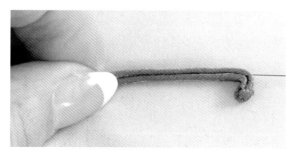

Figure 53

7. Sew through the fold and the new wrapped double layer of soutache (figure 54).

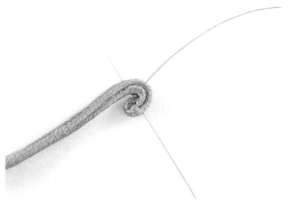

Figure 54

8. Begin to turn the work clockwise and work as in **Simple Spiral** (figure 55).

Figure 55

Ladders

Ladders—lines of beads captured between two stacks—have many variations and uses. But they can all be defined as having one each of four different attributes:

Secured versus Independent

Secured ladders are formed by attaching a new stack to a stack that has already been secured. Because the secured stack cannot change shape, the shape of the resulting ladder is informed by the shape of the secured stack.

Independent ladders are worked entirely in the hand. They can be straight, curved, or shaped in any direction because they are not attached to anything (figure 56).

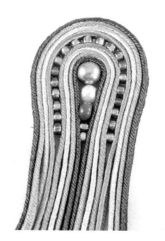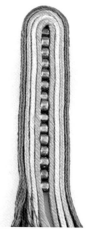

Figure 56

Parallel versus Graduated

Parallel ladders are formed when all the beads in the ladder are the same size, effectively keeping the stacks the same distance apart at all times.

Graduated ladders are formed when the beads in the ladder either increase, pushing the ladder-sides apart, or decrease, bringing the ladder-sides together (figure 57).

Straight versus Curved

Straight ladders are formed when the distance between stitches is the same on the upper stack and the lower stack.

Curved ladders are formed when the distance between the stitches is longer or shorter in one stack than in the other (figure 59).

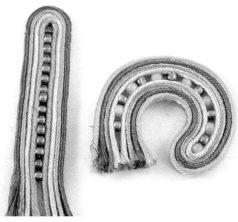

Figure 59

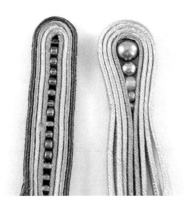

Figure 57

Open versus Closed

Open ladders are formed when the two stacks do not connect to one another.

Closed ladders are formed when the two stacks connect to one another (figure 58).

Note: A ladder can be closed on one end and open on the other (see the center component of figure 58). Ladders can be closed either by sewing the two stacks together (joined) (see the far right component), or a single stack can be wrapped around the first or last bead in a ladder (see the center component).

Making an independent curved ladder. Making a **secured curved** ladder is very easy because the secured stack around which you are building the ladder dictates the shape and the curve just happens naturally. Making an independent curved ladder is a little more challenging because you really have to think about angling the needle as you sew through the upper stack. Follow the directions below to get the hang of making these incredibly versatile elements.

1. Cut the desired number of pieces of soutache the desired lengths and colors (you can make your stack as large as you like, as long as it's at least two layers thick and the length should be twice as long as you want your ladder to be—in this example, I've used four layers).

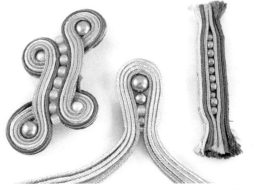

Figure 58

2. Prepare the thread and **align and stack** the soutache. Sew up through the center of the stack. Fold the stack over the knot and orient the work so that the fold is pointed toward your dominant hand. Sew up though the lower stack very close to the fold (figure 60).

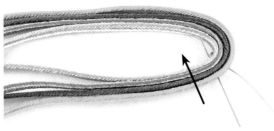

Figure 60

3. Pick up a bead. (You can make ladders with virtually any size of regularly shaped bead—11° through 6° seed beads, 2 mm through 6 mm round beads, and hex beads all work well. For this example, I've used 8° seed beads). Sew up through the upper stack directly above where the thread exited the lower stack (figure 61).

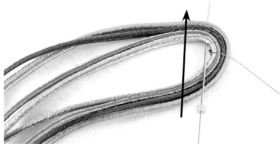

Figure 61

4. Retrace the thread path through the upper stack, bead, and lower stack (figure 62).

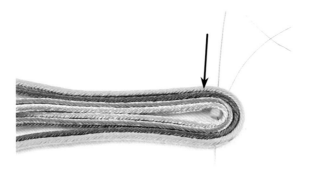

Figure 62

5. Working from right to left, make one **invisible shaping stitch** so that the thread exits one bead-width away from where the thread entered the lower stack (figure 63).

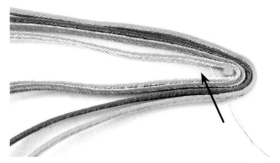

Figure 63

6. Pick up a bead. Sew up through the upper stack. *Do not sew straight up as shown in figure 64 as this will result in a straight ladder.* Rather, angle your needle 45° so that thread enters the upper stack one-and-a-half bead widths away from where the thread last exited the upper stack (figure 65).

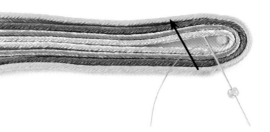

Figure 64

Figure 65

7. Retrace the thread path through the upper stack, bead, and lower stack (figure 66) adding a slight amount of thread tension.

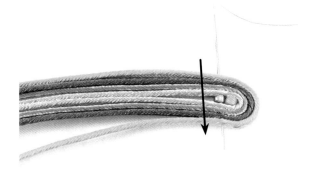

Figure 66

8. Repeat steps 5 through 7 until you have created a curved stack of the desired length.

Note: In step 6, if you sew up at a narrower angle, your curve will be softer or less pronounced. If you sew at a wider angle entering the upper stack farther away from the previous bead, your curve will be tighter.

Special ladders. Although the techniques used for the following ladders are quite basic, the results include unique shapes, paths, and textures that can add a lot of interest to your work.

Note: All of the techniques described below can be altered in terms of numbers of strands of braid in the stacks as well as the bead sizes and types. My instructions are written as photographed, but don't be afraid to change it up.

Chain stitch

Variations on this pattern appear in many soutache artists' work. It makes great bands for necklaces and bracelets. But because these elements are rarely fully backed, the trick to making them well is making sure that the beads don't pop out from between the braids and that the joins do not open up. Use this technique to make sturdy, long-lasting elements for your precious creations.

1. Cut three 8-inch (20.3 cm) lengths of soutache in your choice of colors. **Prepare the thread** and **align and stack** the soutache and sew up through the center of the stack at the rib. Fold the stack over the knot (figure 67).

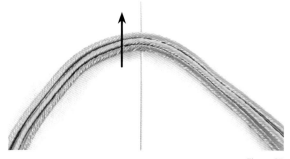

Figure 67

2. Working from left to right, make one **shaping stitch** (figure 68).

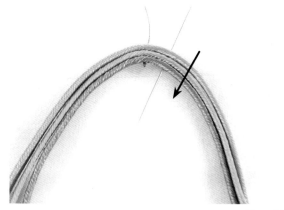

Figure 68

3. Pick up a 4 mm pearl and sew through the left stack directly across from where the thread exited the right stack (figure 69).

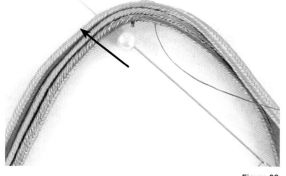

Figure 69

4. Retrace the thread path through the left stack, bead, and right stack (figure 70).

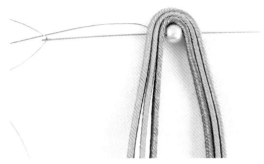

Figure 70

5. Working from top to bottom, make an **invisible shaping stitch** through the right stack (the thread should exit close to the bead) and sew through the innermost strand of the left-hand stack (figure 71).

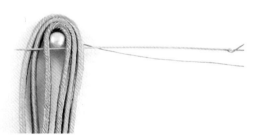

Figure 71

6. Sew back through the left innermost strand and the right innermost strand only (stay close to the bead—you may stitch over the previous stitches) (figure 72).

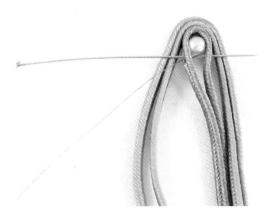

Figure 72

7. Sew back through both the innermost strands and all the left outermost strands (figure 73).

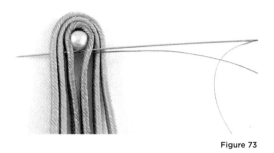

Figure 73

8. Sew back through the left stack and all the right outermost strands (figure 74).

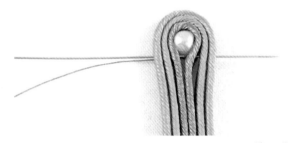

Figure 74

9. Retrace the thread path through the large stack twice, increasing the thread tension with each pass.

10. Split the large stack symmetrically. Working from the top to the bottom, make an invisible shaping stitch so that the thread exits half a bead width away from the join (figure 75).

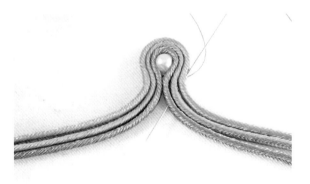

Figure 75

11. Repeat steps 3 through 10 until the chain is the desired length (figure 76).

Figure 76

Swans' heads

Swans' heads are simply very short ladders made of bugle beads. Their shape does suggest a swan's head, but they also make wonderful leaf, petal, and feather shapes.

1. Cut three 8-inch (20.3 cm) lengths of soutache in your choice of colors. **Prepare the thread** and **align and stack** the soutache and sew up through the center of the stack at the rib. Fold the stack over the knot (figure 77).

Figure 77

2. Retrace the thread path through all six strands of braid three times, slightly increasing the thread tension with each pass (figure 78).

Figure 78

3. Split the large stack symmetrically. Sew up through the lower stack so that the thread exits very close to the join (figure 79).

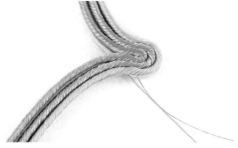

Figure 79

4. Pick up a ¼-inch (6 mm) bugle bead and sew up through the upper stack ¼ inch (6 mm) away from the join (figure 80).

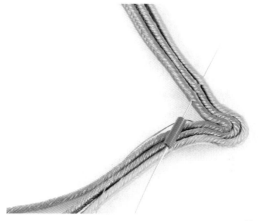

Figure 80

5. Retrace the thread path through the upper stack, bead, and lower stack (figure 81).

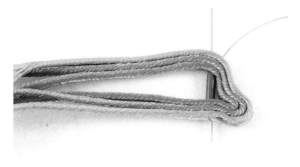

Figure 81

6. Working from right to left, make one **invisible shaping stitch** so that the thread exits the lower stack half a bead width away from the bugle bead (figure 82).

Figure 82

7. Pick up another bead and sew straight up through the upper stack (figure 83).

Figure 83

8. Sew down through the upper stack, the first bugle bead, and the lower stack (figure 84).

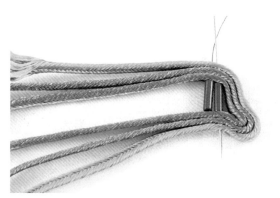

Figure 84

9. Make one invisible shaping stitch so that the thread exits the lower stack half a bead width away from the second bugle bead (figure 85).

Figure 85

10. Pick up another bead and sew straight up through the upper stack (figure 86).

Figure 86

11. Sew down through the upper stack, the second bugle bead, and the lower stack (figure 87).

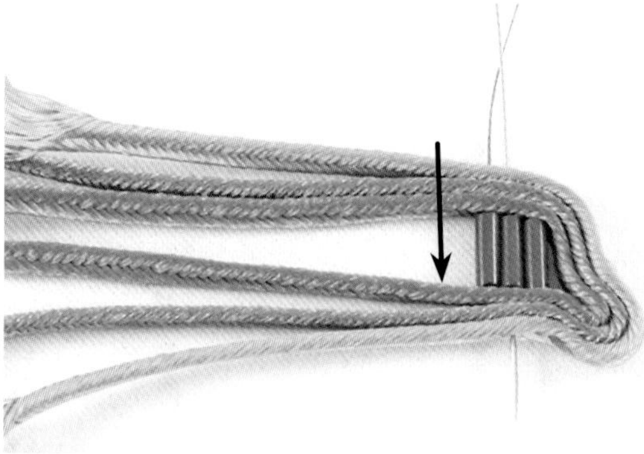

Figure 87

12. Following steps 9 through 11, add a fourth bugle bead, sewing down through the third bugle bead as in step 11 (figure 88).

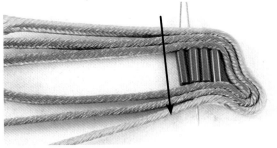

Figure 88

13. Sew up through the bottom stack, the fourth bugle bead, and the upper stack (figure 89).

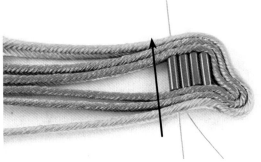

Figure 89

14. Bring the lower stack up to meet the upper stack near the top of the fourth bugle bead. Sew through both upper and lower stacks (figure 90).

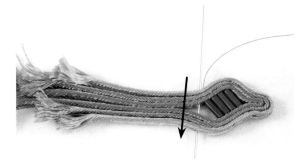

Figure 90

15. Retrace the thread path twice, adding a slight amount of thread tension with each pass (figure 91).

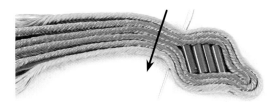

Figure 91

16. The "neck" of the swan can be curved and held in shape with invisible shaping stitches or sculpted into other designs (figure 92).

Figure 92

Rolling waves

The rolling waves pattern starts as **secured ladder** worked around a small, round area of the work like a lollipop that is attached to a larger core component or an ended stack that is connected to a larger component. The new stack soon doubles back on itself, however, creating a series of semicircular ladders that seem to overlap.

1. Determine the area around which you want to begin the rolling waves pattern. (In my example, I'm going to start it around the ended stack at the top of my core component and work it from left to right around the core component) (figure 93).

Figure 93

2. Cut two 12-inch (30.5 cm) lengths of soutache. **Prepare the thread.** Turn the work over. (It is easier to stitch the rolling waves pattern from the back of the work.) Sew into the work so that the thread exits the soutache at the rib near the base of the ended stack. On the front of the work, this would be the left side (figure 94).

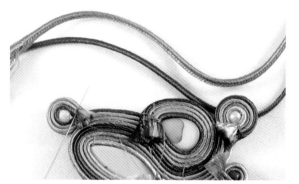

Figure 94

3. Pick up an 8° seed bead and sew through the new stack approximately 1½ inches (3.8 cm) from one end of the new stack (figure 95).

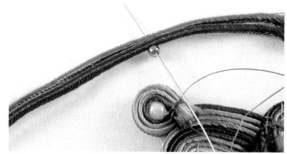

Figure 95

4. Begin working a **ladder** around the shape of the ended stack using 8° seed beads (figure 96).

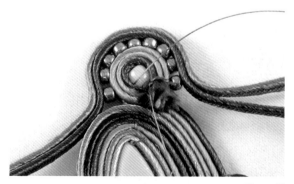

Figure 96

5. When you reach the base of the shape you are surrounding, **set** the last stitch and **retrace the thread path** once or twice (figure 97).

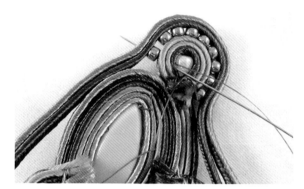

Figure 97

6. Anchor the working stack to the core component shape by sewing through the working stack and into the secured stack surrounding the core component. The thread can exit on an angle out of the back of the secured stack once it's gone through at least two or three layers. It is not important to sew through the entire stack (figure 98).

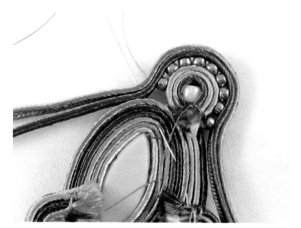

Figure 98

7. Retrace the thread path so that the thread exits the working stack where it joined the secured stack of the core component (figure 99).

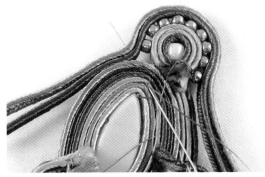

Figure 99

8. Pick up a 4 mm bead (figure 100). Sew through the stack where the bead's hole naturally meets the stack. Follow the directions for **ending a stack**, including **tacking** the working stack in place behind the work, but *do not* whip or snip off the remaining working stack (figure 101).

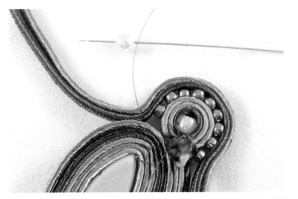

Figure 100

Figure 101

9. Fold the working stack back on itself. Sew up through the stack near the fold, making sure the fold stays behind the work (figure 102).

Figure 102

10. Pick up an 8° seed bead and sew through the upper stack (figure 103).

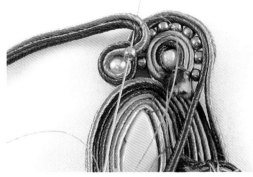

Figure 103

11. Following steps 4 through 8, make a ladder around the previously added 4 mm bead (figure 104).

Figure 104

12. Repeat steps 7 through 11 until you have created as many rolling waves as desired. When you finish the last ladder, end the stack around a 4 mm bead (figure 105).

Figure 105

13. Pull the thread across the back of the work and secure the first part of the working stack to the core shape (figure 106). End the stack around a 4 mm bead (figure 107).

Figure 106

Figure 107

Flame stitch

This technique is unusual because it is essentially worked from the outside in. Each short graduated ladder is followed by the addition of a new stack. Pieces made with this method have a lot of drama and movement because the graduating lines pull your eye around the work.

1. Cut two 8-inch (20.3 cm) lengths of soutache. **Prepare the thread** and **align and stack** the soutache. Sew up through center of the stack at the rib (figure 108).

Figure 108

2. Fold the stack over the knot (figure 109).

Figure 109

3. Sew up through all four layers of the braid very close to the fold (figure 110).

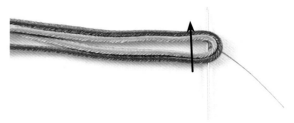

Figure 110

4. Retrace the thread path three times (figure 111).

Figure 111

5. Split the stack symmetrically. Sew up through the lower stack very close to the fold (figure 112).

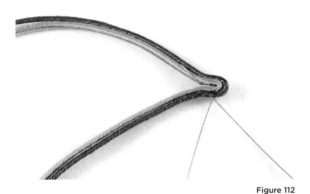

Figure 112

6. Pick up an 11° seed bead. Sew up through the upper stack (figure 113).

Figure 113

7. Retrace the thread path through the upper stack, bead, and lower stack (figure 114).

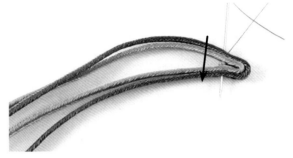

Figure 114

8. Working from right to left, make one **invisible shaping stitch** so that the thread exits the lower stack one bead width away from where thread last entered it (figure 115).

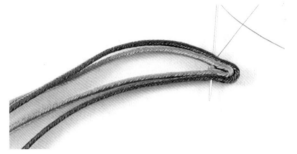

Figure 115

9. Following steps 6 through 8, add an 8° and a 6° seed bead.

10. Working from right to left, make one **invisible shaping stitch** so that the thread exits above the lower stack one bead width away from where the thread last entered it. Finish with the thread exiting above the lower stack (figure 116).

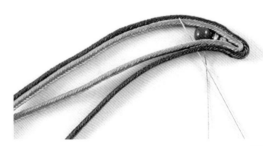

Figure 116

Note: Using the spacing technique described in **Making an Independent Curved Ladder**, you can curve this piece as much or as little as you like.

11. Cut two 8-inch (20.3 cm) lengths of soutache and **align and stack** them. Fold the stack in half and sew through all four layers of braid very close to the fold (figure 117).

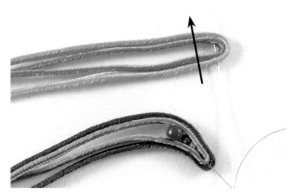

Figure 117

12. Sew up through the upper stack of first stack pair (figure 118). The second stack pair is now nestled inside the first stack pair making a large eight-layer stack (figure 119).

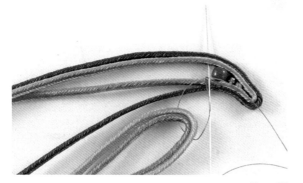

Figure 118

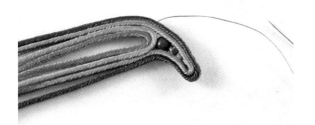

Figure 119

13. Retrace the thread path three times, adding a slight amount of thread tension with each pass (figure 120).

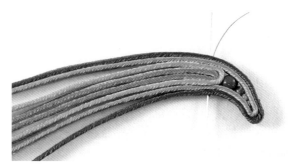

Figure 120

14. Following steps 5 through 9, add another graduated ladder composed of an 11°, an 8°, and a 6° seed bead (figure 121).

Figure 121

15. Repeat steps 10 through 14, curving the component until the component reaches the desired size and shape (figure 122).

Figure 122

16. As you work, the outermost layers of the working stacks will become too short to be incorporated into the flame stitch technique. When that happens, sew through the work at the point you'd like to end those layers (figure 123). Pick up a 4 mm bead. Split away the layers you'd like to end, forming a new stack (figure 124). Sew through the stack where the bead hole naturally meets the stack. End the stack (figure 125).

17. You can pick up where you left off with the flame stitch technique, continuing to enlarge the component and stopping now and again to end outer layers as needed (figure 126).

Figure 126

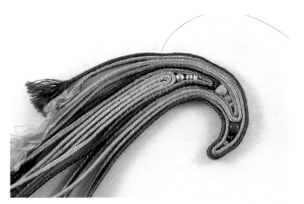

Figure 123

Fork stitch

In many ways, this is the opposite of the **flame stitch**. As new stacks are added, rather than consolidating them into a larger stack, the new stacks branch off, creating new **ladders**. This stitch can be very consistent and planned, or it can wander organically. Your choices will determine whether you end up with something fractal and fernlike, or wildly random like coral.

1. Cut two 8-inch (20.3 cm) lengths of soutache. **Align and stack** them. Following the directions for **Making an Independent Curved Ladder**, make a ladder of seven 8° seed beads (figure 127).

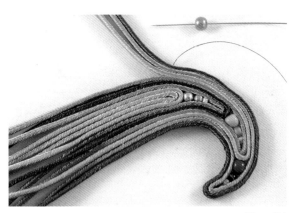

Figure 124

Figure 125

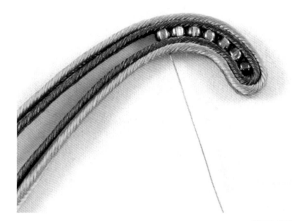

Figure 127

2. Sew up through the lower stack. Separate the upper and lower stacks. Cut two more 8-inch (20.3 cm) lengths of soutache. Align and stack them. Fold the stack in half so the outer color braid is the same as the inner color braids of the ladder you just made. Place the fold between the stacks of the ladder (figure 128).

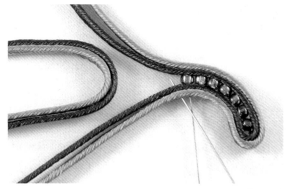

Figure 128

3. Pick up an 8° seed bead and begin making a ladder between the lower stack of the first ladder and the lower stack of the new folded stack (figure 129).

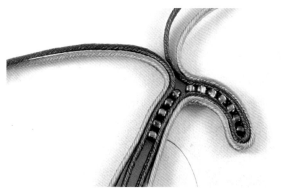

Figure 129

4. Retrace the thread path through the stack, bead, and stack twice. Trim the thread (figure 130).

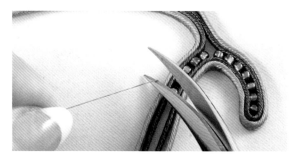

Figure 130

5. Prepare the thread and **bury the knot** by sewing through the bead and the stack close to the working stacks (these are comprised of the upper stack from the first ladder and upper stack of the new folded stack (figure 131).

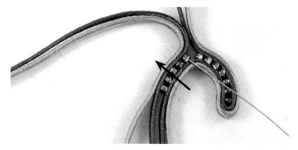

Figure 131

6. Create a ladder between the two working stacks (figure 132).

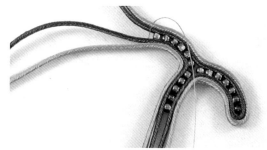

Figure 132

7. Continue separating the stacks by inserting new folded stacks and creating new ladders of varying lengths and curves. Secure and trim the thread as needed so you can work on different ends of the piece (figure 133).

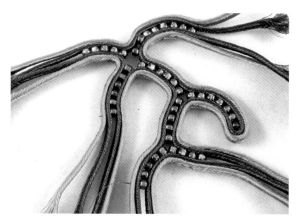

Figure 133

8. As you work, some stacks will become too short to continue. Sew through the work at the point at which you would like to end a stack and pick up a bead, such as a 6°, a 4 mm, or a 6 mm (it's fun to use beads of varying sizes in this technique!), sew through the stack where the bead hole naturally meets the stack, and **end the stack** (figure 134).

Figure 134

Incorporating Larger Elements

When you make a lollipop around a small or medium-sized bead (2 mm to 6 mm), you probably find the bead sits snug and happy in its little soutache frame. But what if you'd like your soutache to surround something larger—like a bigger bead, a button, or a cabochon? This section gives you instructions for dealing with large and oddly shaped items.

Large beads. The larger the bead you're working with, the greater the likelihood it's going to want to "spin" inside the soutache frame when you're making a lollipop (figure 135). And even if you can coax it into staying put while you work it, there's a pretty good chance it's going to try and move again later while you're trying to attach new elements to its secured stack. Here are two methods for taming frisky beads.

Figure 135

Net the back

This is a good solution for beads that are just large enough to start to cause trouble.

1. Make a lollipop.

2. Working from the back, sew into the secured stack surrounding the bead.

3. Sew back into the secured stack and pull your thread across the back of the work. Sew into the secured stack at another location.

4. Repeat step 3 in a random, crisscross pattern until there is enough "net" to keep the bead from spinning in its frame (figure 136).

Figure 136

Sew the bead onto the foundation

This is the best solution for very large beads or beads with very rounded or faceted backs.

1. Put a drop of washable fabric glue onto a piece of beading foundation (the piece of beading foundation should be larger than the bead).

2. Press the bead into the glue and allow it to dry completely (figure 137).

Figure 137

3. Prepare the thread.

4. Sew up through the beading foundation very close to one of the bead holes (figure 138).

Figure 138

5. Sew through the bead.

6. Sew down through the beading foundation on the other side.

7. Repeat steps 4 through 6 several times to secure the bead. If the bead has a rounded or faceted back, be sure to allow the stitches to flare out of the bead hole by sewing up or down slightly to the right or left of the hole (figure 139). This will help stabilize the bead.

Figure 139

8. Embellish or trim and add soutache around the beading foundation as described in **Working off the Beading Foundation** (figure 140).

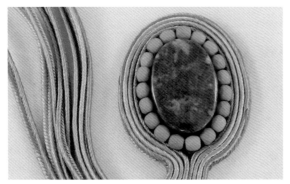

Figure 140

Tall beads

Some beads are a workable diameter, but their height makes them vulnerable in the finished work—a little tippy and inclined to fall at odd angles. Spike beads are great in soutache and bead embroidery and a perfect example of how those tall beads—with a little extra attention—can add a whole new dimension to your work.

1. Work the spike bead into your design as you would any other 4 mm or 6 mm bead (here, I've chosen to incorporate the bead into the work with a **one-sided join**) (figure 141).

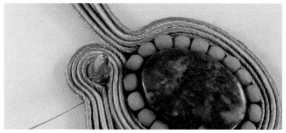

Figure 141

Note: Even though the bead is secure in the work, you can see how easily it tips to the side (figure 142).

Figure 142

2. Sew into the secured stack so the thread exits the work in the back (figure 143).

Figure 143

3. Sew up through the work (you will not be in the rib of the stack) so that thread exits close to the bead (figure 144).

Figure 144

4. Following the directions for **Cabochons** and treating the secured stack as you would the beading foundation, create a peyote-stitch bezel consisting of a base row, a row one of 11° seed beads, and a row two of 15° seed beads (figure 145).

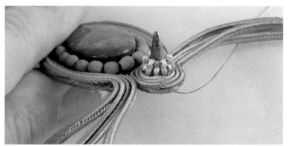

Figure 145

Cabochons. Cabochons are elements with flat backs and no holes. While some artists choose to rely solely on jewelry glue to hold their cabochons in place, I recommend creating a mechanical bond by working a **peyote-stitch bezel**. If you are unfamiliar with this technique, use the two-color method below until you gain confidence.

1. Following the directions for **Sew the Bead onto the Foundation**, use a dab of washable fabric glue to adhere the cabochon to a piece of beading foundation.

2. Following the directions for **Backstitch 2**, use two colors of 11° seed beads to surround the cabochon with a row of backstitch 2. Alternating between these two colors will ensure you complete the ring of beads (from here on called the base row) with an even number of beads (figure 146).

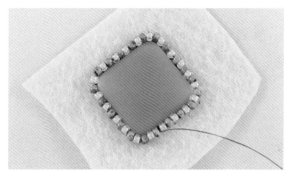

Figure 146

3. Sew through the first bead in the base row and "step up" to the next row by picking up an 11° seed bead the same color as the first bead in base row.

4. Sew over the second bead in the base row and through the third bead in the base row (figure 147). You should be sewing through a bead of the same color you just added.

Figure 147

5. Pick up another 11° seed bead. Sew over the fourth bead in the base row and through the fifth (figure 148). Notice the two beads you just added are each sitting on top of the alternate color beads (figure 149).

Figure 148

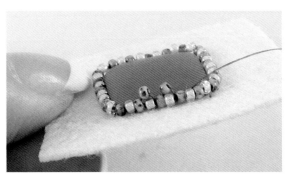

Figure 149

6. Following step 5, add an 11° seed bead on top of every other bead in the base row (figure 150). The thread now should be exiting the first bead in the base row. This completes row one.

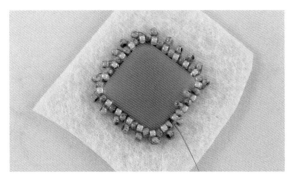

Figure 150

7. Step up by again by sewing through the first bead in row one (figure 151).

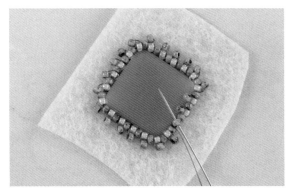

Figure 151

8. Pick up a 15° seed bead. Sew through the second bead in row one. The 15° seed bead now sits between the first two beads of row one (figure 152).

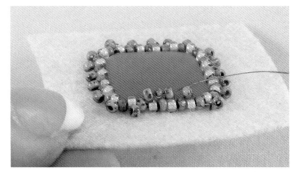

Figure 152

9. Continue following step 8 until there is a 15° seed bead sitting between each pair of 11° seed beads in row one. This completes row two.

Note: If your cabochon is taller or has steeper sides, you may need to make a taller bezel. You would make row two using 11° seed beads after which you would step up by sewing through the first bead in row two and work row three like row one. If the bezel is then high enough to close, row four would be worked with the 15° seed beads. If more height is needed, continue working with 11° seed beads for rows four and five and 15° seed beads for row six.

10. Sew through row one and row two adding thread tension to tighten the ring of beads. This ring forms the "collar" that holds the cabochon in place (figure 153).

Figure 153

11. Sew down through the bezel and the beading foundation (figure 154). Take a couple of **shallow stitches** on the back and trim the thread.

Figure 154

12. Embellish or trim and add soutache around the beading foundation as described in **Working off the Beading Foundation** (figure 155).

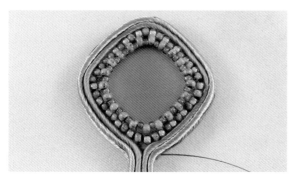

Figure 155

Buttons. Buttons both old and new can make beautiful additions to your work. Buttons with either two or four holes can easily be stitched down to a piece of beading foundation and worked just like a large bead. The holes even give you opportunities for further embellishment, but what about buttons with shanks? These are often long enough that they would either push the button up off your work or cause an unsightly lump on the back. Many shanks are made of glass or are an otherwise integral part of the button. And although some buttons have shanks that can be clipped off easily (in which case you would work the button like a cabochon), the underside of the button may be concave, leaving little surface area for glue to adhere the button to the beading foundation. Here's how to handle buttons with shanks.

1. Prepare the thread.

2. Cut two pieces of beading foundation slightly larger than the button.

3. Fold one piece in half and make a small snip across the center of the fold (figure 156).

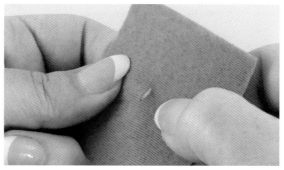

Figure 156

4. This beautiful Czech button has a long metal shank and a hollow back. Sink the button shank into the snip (figure 157).

Figure 157

5. Sew though the beading foundation on one side of the shank, through the shank, and through foundation on other side of the shank.

6. Whipstitch several times, firmly securing the shank to the beading foundation (figure 158). Trim the thread.

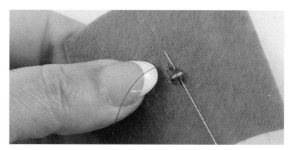

Figure 158

7. Fold the second piece of beading foundation in half. Cut a small inverted V across the center of the fold, making a diamond-shaped cutout when the foundation is unfolded (figure 159).

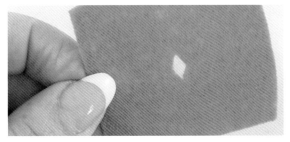

Figure 159

8. Dab a small amount of washable fabric glue around the diamond shape.

9. Press the shank into the cutout (figure 160). Allow the glue to dry completely.

Figure 160

10. Embellish or trim and add soutache around the beading foundation as described in **Working off the Beading Foundation** (figure 161).

Figure 161

Irregularly shaped elements. Sometimes we find something wonderful that's neither fish nor fowl nor good red herring. It might have no holes so it's not a bead. It's got crazy edges so it's almost impossible to build a bezel around. Maybe it's even got a totally wonky front or back surface. Chances are, we've got about eight dozen things in our stash that would look just as great and be a heck of a lot easier to work with, but nooo . . . it's pretty . . . and we want it. So what do we do? As I see it, there are two challenges here: The first is getting our precious thing secured so it won't fall off. The second is to get it into some sort of workable shape so we can attach soutache.

Secure the Element

1. Cut a piece of beading foundation a little larger than your element. Using a toothpick, put a small dab of jewelry glue onto the foundation and press your element into the glue (figure 162). Allow it to dry completely.

Figure 162

2. Prepare the thread.

3. Sew up through the beading foundation very close to the edge of the element (figure 163).

Figure 163

4. Pick up a run of seed beads. I'm using 15°, 11°, and a few 8° seed beads, but you can use whatever feels proportional to the element.

5. Draw the run of beads across the element to see what angle is pleasing to you and to test for length (figure 164). Add more beads if necessary.

Figure 164

6. Sew over the element at desired angles and through the beading foundation close to the element (figure 165).

Figure 165

7. Sew up through the beading foundation at a new location close to the element.

8. Follow steps 4 and 5 until the new run of beads intersects the first (figure 166). Sew through four of five of the beads in the middle of the first run (figure 167). Pick up more beads, pull them across the element at a new angle, and sew down through the beading foundation.

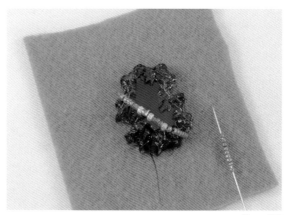

Figure 166

Figure 167

9. Follow steps 7 and 8 at random angles, creating a "cage" of beads (figure 168).

Figure 168

Reshape the Element

1. Using a drafter's inking template, select a more regular shape to fit around the irregular element (figure 169). Trace the shape around your element (figure 170).

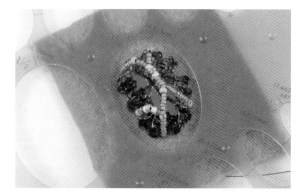

Figure 169

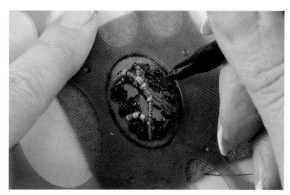

Figure 170

Note: You can choose any shape or even draw your shape freehand, but keep the size of the shape as close as possible to the general size of your element.

2. Prepare the thread.

3. Sew up through the beading foundation very close to the element.

4. Pick up a run of seed beads just long enough to extend to your tracing line (figure 171). I used 15°s because my element is small and there's not a lot of area to cover.

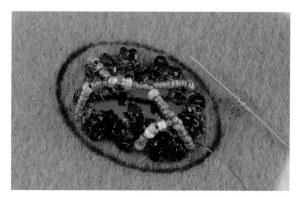

Figure 171

5. Sew down through the beading foundation (figure 172).

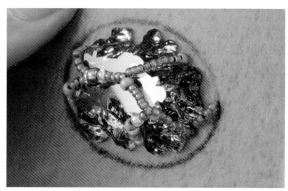

Figure 172

6. Sew up through beading foundation very close to the beginning of the last line of beads. Follow steps 4 and 5 to create a second line of beads (figure 173).

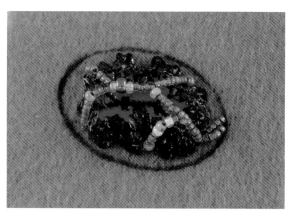

Figure 173

7. Continue following step 6 for two or three more rows (figure 174).

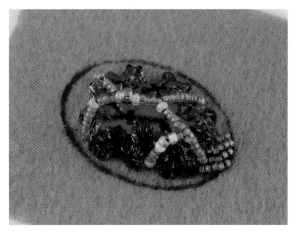

Figure 174

8. Every three or four rows, turn and work the rows in a different direction. Continue working this way until all of the area between the element and the trace line is filled in (figure 175).

Figure 175

Note: This technique is a bead embroidery stitch sometimes referred to as "lazy stitch." If you love traditional bead embroidery, you will be pleased to see just how well it mixes with soutache. While several techniques are called out in this book, there are entire volumes dedicated to the craft that are filled with creative ideas you can incorporate into your work.

9. Trim and add soutache around the beading foundation as described in **Working off the Beading Foundation** (figure 176).

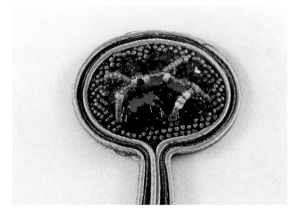

Figure 176

Working off the beading foundation. Whether you've chosen to work with a large bead, a cabochon, a button, or an irregular element, the common denominator here is they're all attached to beading foundation. You can use this opportunity for further embellishment, or you can simply trim away the foundation and begin attaching your soutache.

Embellishing with backstitch 2. If an element is particularly tall, it's sometimes nice to create a bit of a transition by surrounding it with a ring of slightly shorter beads. Backstitch 2 is a common bead embroidery technique and one worth learning since it's how you make the base row for a peyote-stitch bezel.

1. Prepare the thread.

2. Sew up through the beading foundation very close to the bead, cabochon, button, or other element (from here, we'll refer to this as the "large bead") (figure 177).

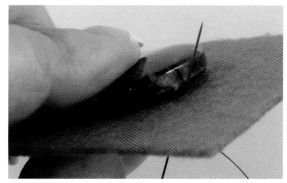

Figure 177

3. Pick up two beads. (I used 4 mm fire-polished beads, but you can use any of a variety of beads including, but not limited to, round beads, pearls, or 6° or 8° seed beads.)

4. Working counterclockwise, sew down through beading foundation very close to large bead. Be sure you make a stitch that is actually longer than the two beads require (figure 178).

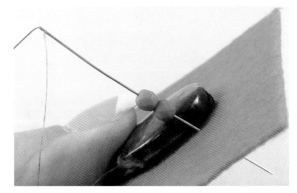

Figure 178

Note: Always making these stitches longer than necessary will ensure you don't accidentally make your stitch too short and cause your beads to bunch up or "inchworm."

5. Push the beads back to the beginning of the stitch (figure 179).

Figure 179

6. Sew up through the beading foundation so the thread exits between the first and second beads (figure 180).

Figure 180

7. Sew through the second bead.

8. Pick up two more beads (figure 181).

Figure 181

9. Following steps 4 and 5, sew down through the beading foundation (figure 182), then push the beads backward.

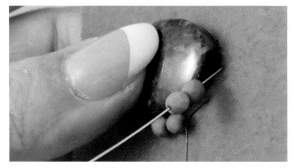

Figure 182

10. Sew up through the beading foundation so the thread exits between the last and second-to-last beads (figure 183).

Figure 183

11. Sew through the last bead (figure 184).

Figure 184

12. Continue following steps 8 through 11 until the large bead is surrounded by a ring of smaller beads (figure 185).

Figure 185

13. Sew through the ring of beads once or twice, adding a slight amount of thread tension to round and tighten ring and to fill in bead holes a little bit (figure 186).

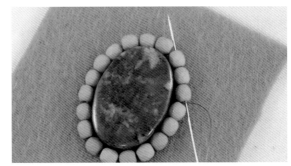

Figure 186

14. Sew down into beading foundation (figure 187). Take a couple of **shallow stitches** on the back of the work. Trim thread.

Figure 187

Adding soutache around beading foundation

1. Trim the beading foundation away from the work. Be careful not to overtrim—approximately ¹⁄₃₂ inch (1 mm) of beading foundation should be visible when the work is viewed from the front (figure 188). Take your time here—keep your cutting smooth and even. Because the soutache is applied directly to the edge of the beading foundation, any jigs or jags are going to telegraph through the stack and inform the shape of your finished work.

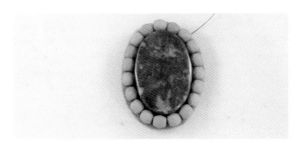

Figure 188

2. Prepare the thread.

3. Working from the back, sew into the beading foundation on a slight angle so the thread exits the edge of the beading foundation *at the center top of the work* (figure 189). The needle should come right through the edge—not the top or bottom; as it is passing through, it should look like a bookmark sticking out of a book (figure 190).

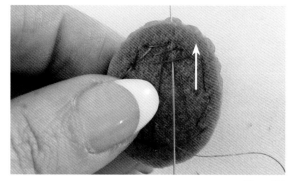

Figure 189

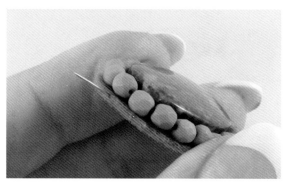

Figure 190

4. Cut four 8-inch (20.3 cm) lengths of soutache. (The length of the soutache you cut and the number of pieces will vary from project to project; this is simply what I used for the example.)

5. Sew up through the center of one piece of soutache at the rib.

6. Let the soutache slide down the thread. The rib should rest against the edge of the beading foundation.

7. Working from right to left, sew down into the rib of the soutache and the edge of the beading foundation, angling the needle slightly so the thread exits the back of the beading foundation (figure 191).

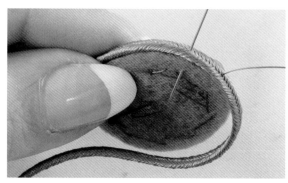

Figure 191

8. Working from right to left, sew into the beading foundation, out of the edge of beading foundation, and through the soutache at the rib (figure 192).

Figure 192

9. Following steps 7 and 8, continue attaching soutache around the work until you reach the center bottom.

Note: These stitches can be pretty large. This shape is about 1½ inches (3.8 cm) at its longest, and I attached the soutache from top to bottom with about six stitches. Don't waste your time making forty-three itty-bitty stitches.

10. If your thread is exiting the soutache, sew back into the soutache and the beading foundation so the thread is exiting the back of the work. Pull your thread across the back of the work and sew back into the beading foundation, out of the edge of the beading foundation, and out of the soutache at the rib (figure 193).

Figure 193

11. Working clockwise, follow steps 7 through 9 to secure the soutache around the other side of the work (figure 194).

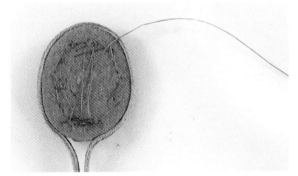

Figure 194

12. Following step 10, bring your thread back to the top center of the work so the thread is exiting the soutache. **Align and stack** the remaining three lengths of soutache; the strands should be oriented in the same direction as the already-secured braid.

13. Sew through the center of the stack at the rib.

14. Following steps 6 through 11, secure the stack around both sides of the work, being sure to sew through the new stack, the secured piece of soutache, and through the edge of the beading foundation with each stitch (figure 195).

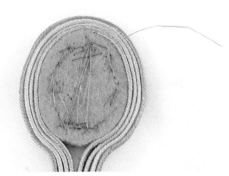

Figure 195

15. Sew into the back of the work so the thread exits the beading foundation at the center bottom of work (figure 196).

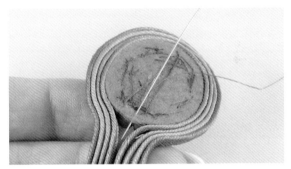

Figure 196

16. Join the stacks with a **two-sided join** (figure 197).

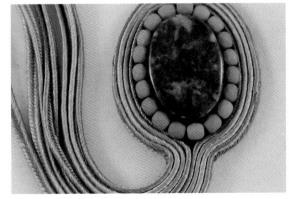

Figure 197

Note: Working the soutache around one half of the shape and then the other is the best way to make sure you end up with working stacks of equal lengths. This gives you maximum design flexibility as you carry on with your work.

Multi-piece Elements

Sometimes one bead just isn't enough. Maybe you don't have a bead that's quite the right size or you're looking for an element with more visual interest. In such cases, it can be effective to combine beads (or beads and findings) so that—aesthetically—they behave like a single element.

SuperDuos. A SuperDuo is just one of the many wonderful "two-hole" beads that have become available in the past few years. They are particularly useful because they stack up like bricks resulting in an interesting, quilted texture, and there are many ways to use them. For most of the applications in this book, we will make diamond-shaped motifs the size of which are determined by the number of vertical rows that are either increasing or decreasing in height.

1. After any join, split stack symmetrically. Sew through lower stack so that thread exits close to Join (figure 198).

Figure 198

2. Pick up one SuperDuo (figure 199).

Figure 199

3. Sew through upper stack directly above where the thread exited lower stack. **This completes the first row** (figure 200).

Figure 200

4. Increase. Working from right to left, sew down through upper stack so that the thread exits in line with second hole of the SuperDuo (figure 201).

Figure 201

5. Pick up a second SuperDuo. Sew through second hole of first SuperDuo (figure 202).

Figure 202

6. Pick up a third SuperDuo. Sew through lower stack (figure 203). **This completes the second row.**

Figure 203

7. Decrease. Sew up through lower stack so the thread exits in line with the second hole of third SuperDuo. Sew through second hole of third SuperDuo (figure 204).

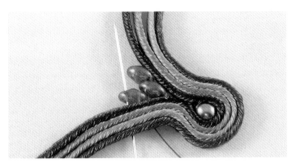

Figure 204

8. Pick up a fourth SuperDuo and sew through the second hole of second SuperDuo and the upper Stack (figure 205). **This completes third row.**

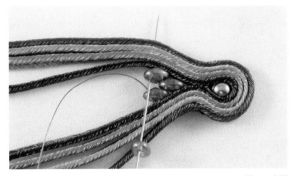

Figure 205

9. Sew down through the upper stack so the thread exits in line with the second hole of the fourth SuperDuo. Sew through second hole of fourth SuperDuo and the lower stack (figure 206).

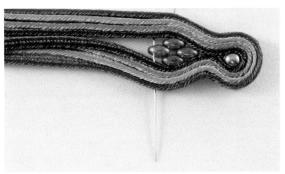

Figure 206

10. Working from right to left, sew up through the lower stack and upper stack (figure 207).

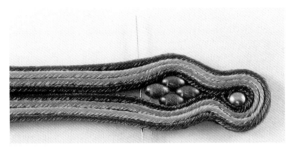

Figure 207

11. Set the stitch by retracing thread path twice.

Note: This is a four SuperDuo motif but—if you continued to increase the number of beads in each row—you can make larger and larger shapes. This NineSuperDuo motif increases to three beads in the middle row before decreasing to two and then one. (figure 208) A 16 motif increases to four beads in the middle row before decreasing (figure 209).

Figure 208

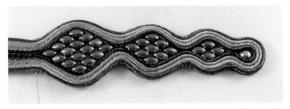

Figure 209

Other Elements

Soutache is an incredibly versatile medium, so it plays well with others. The following is a list of fun ingredients I routinely incorporate into work and some suggestions on how to use them. It is by no means a comprehensive list since there are many clever ways to incorporate these and myriad other things. Some of the techniques fall more solidly under the heading of traditional bead embroidery, but there is a lot of overlap between the two craft forms.

Backgrounds

Soutache and bead embroidery each can stand on their own, but they can also be applied on top of beading foundation, and more beading can be done around it. The items in the list below are most often applied on top of the beading foundation to add another layer of interest and detail.

Fish leather. Fish leather (figure 210)— a product of the tilapia industry—is exactly what it sounds like: leather made from fish skin. It can be dyed brilliant colors, and it's not nearly as heavy as cowhide and other traditional leather. It still can be quite tough, so use larger scissors to cut shapes and use as little glue as possible.

Figure 210

1. Use larger scissors to cut a shape out of the fish leather (figure 211).

Figure 211

2. Apply a small amount of glue to the back of the leather and spread it thinly. Do not spread glue all the way to the edges (figure 212). This will make it easier to sew through the leather later.

Figure 212

3. Press it in the desired location on your beading foundation. Allow to dry completely (figure 213).

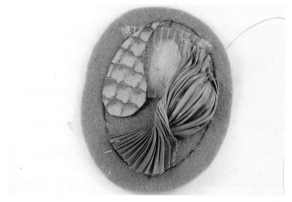

Figure 213

4. Prepare the thread.

5. Secure the fish leather by sewing up through the beading foundation very close to the edge of the leather (figure 214).

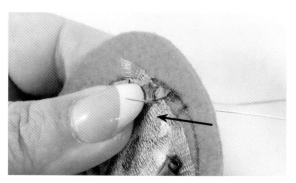

Figure 214

6. Pulling the thread just over the edge of the leather, sew down through just the leather and the beading foundation (figure 215).

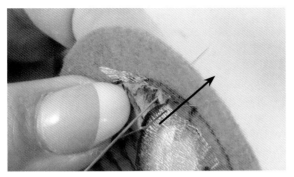

Figure 215

7. Working your way around the leather, repeat steps 4 and 5 every ½ inch (1.3 cm) and at any corner.

It is always easier to sew down through the fish leather and beading foundation than it is to sew up through the beading foundation and the fish leather. If the leather is hard to sew through, try twisting your needle as your push it. Failing that, push with flat-nose pliers, holding your needle as close as possible to the point to avoid breaking it.

Shibori ribbon. Shibori ribbon is silk ribbon that has been hand-dyed and pleated. As the pleats are fanned open, different colors are revealed in the valleys (the low points in the folds) (figure 216).

Figure 216

1. Trim off any frayed or raveled edges.

2. Prepare the thread.

3. Lay the ribbon on the beading foundation.

4. Starting at a corner, secure the ribbon with **tacking stitches**. Sew up through the beading foundation and the ribbon so the thread exits a valley. Sew back down very close to where thread last exited, making the smallest possible stitch (figure 217).

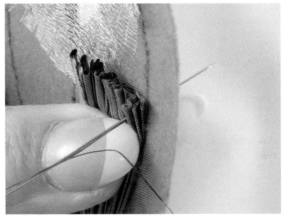

Figure 217

5. Fan and sculpt the ribbon at random, securing with tacking stitches (figure 218). Don't be afraid to twist it or push it up to form swells (figure 219). If you've created a lifted area and want it to maintain its volume, cut up some scraps of beading foundation and push them under the lifted area of ribbon. You can use the back end of a darning needle to help maneuver them into place (figure 220). Continue tacking (figure 221).

Figure 218

Figure 219

Figure 220

Figure 221

6. Trim the excess shibori ribbon away from your work (figure 222).

Figure 222

WireLace. WireLace (ribbon woven with very fine wires of brass, copper, and/or aluminum) can be stretched and shaped in lots of ways. Part of its beauty is its translucency, so you can stretch it over other materials and simply tack it down at the edges. You can also stretch it across negative spaces. If you'd like to try this process, it's important to address the backing while you work on your design.

1. Determine the shape onto which you want to create your design and either draw or trace it onto a piece of beading foundation. Determine an area you would like to be negative space and draw or trace it onto the design.

2. Trim away the negative space (figure 223).

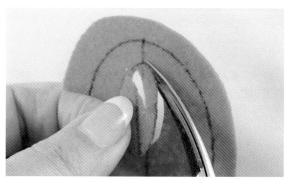

Figure 223

3. Place your shape onto the wrong side of a piece of synthetic suede, making sure there is enough room for the whole shape. Trace the negative shape onto the synthetic suede (figure 224).

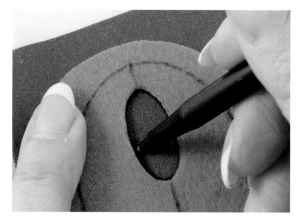

Figure 224

4. Trim the negative space out of the synthetic suede (figure 225).

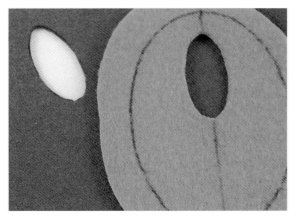

Figure 225

5. Cut a small piece of WireLace and stretch it slightly to the desired texture (figure 226).

Figure 226

6. Lay it over the negative space on the beading foundation and tack it in place (figure 227).

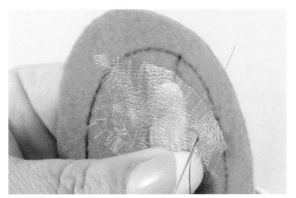

Figure 227

7. After the rest of the design work is done, apply a thin layer of washable fabric glue across back of work. Do not get glue on the WireLace (figure 228). Place the glue side of the work down onto the wrong side of the backing, aligning negative spaces (figure 229). Allow it to dry completely.

Figure 228

Figure 229

Chain and rhinestone chain (cup chain)

Whether you want a subtle metallic gleam or full-on blingification, here are some ingredients and methods for adding sparkle to your work.

Chain. Chain is available in many link styles. You can simply sew it down on your work by stitching over every link or every other link. You can also use beads to hold it in place.

1. Cut a length of chain.

2. Prepare the thread. Lay the first link against your work.

3. Sew up through the beading foundation and the link (figure 230).

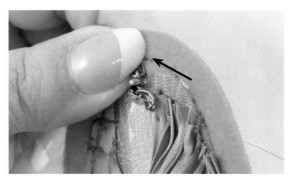

Figure 230

4. Pick up two beads, the first larger than the second. In my example, I've used 6° and 11° seed beads, but you can choose the sizes that are proportional to your chain links.

5. Sew down through the larger bead, the link, any background fabric, and the beading foundation (figure 231).

Figure 231

6. Repeat steps 3 through 5 for each link in the chain (figure 232).

Figure 232

Rhinestone chain (cup chain). There are two methods for incorporating rhinestone chain into your work. The second is more fiddly, but it's a skill worth cultivating as it allows you to work off of a beading foundation.

Working off the beading foundation

1. Prepare the thread.

2. Sew up through the beading foundation very close to the element you wish to surround with rhinestone chain.

3. Lay the chain against your work so the link between the first two rhinestones is next to where your thread is exiting the beading foundation (figure 233).

Figure 233

4. Sew over the link (figure 234).

Figure 234

5. Sew up through the beading foundation so the thread exits between previously applied elements and the next link in the chain. Sew over the link (figure 235).

Figure 235

6. Repeat step 5 until you have nearly surrounded your previously applied work. Determine how many stones will be required to complete your work and use flush cutters to trim off the excess (figure 236). Work as in step 5 to secure the end of chain in place.

Figure 236

Working between stacks. After you have created a soutache lollipop or any other shape, you can attach an additional stack with rhinestone chain captured between the secured stack and the new working stack.

1. Align and stack two or more new lengths of soutache.

2. With thread exiting the secured stack of a previously built shape, sew through the new working stack, but don't allow the new stack to snug tight to the secured stack—leave a short length of exposed thread (figure 237).

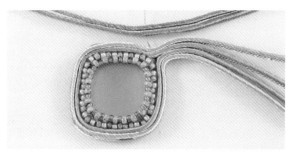

Figure 237

3. Lay the link between the first two stones in the rhinestone chain over the exposed thread (figure 238).

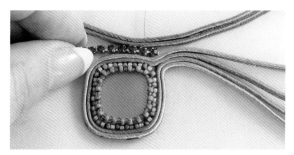

Figure 238

4. Sew back through the working stack, over the link, and into the secured stack (figure 239). Angle the needle slightly so the thread exits the back of work (figure 240).

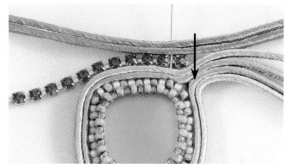

Figure 239

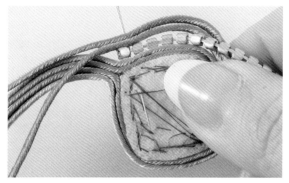

Figure 240

Note: This is one of the only techniques during which I work flat on my work surface. I do this until the first two or three stones are secured into the work, and then I can pick the work up and continue working in my hands as usual.

5. Sew through the secured stack and working stack so the thread passes under the link between the next two stones (figure 241).

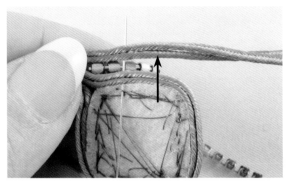

Figure 241

6. Sew through the working stack, over the link and into the secured stack so the thread exits the back of work (figure 242).

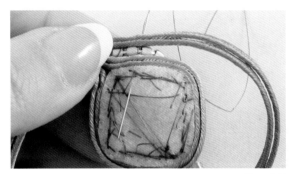

Figure 242

7. Continue working as in steps 5 and 6, capturing the chain between the stacks (figure 243).

Figure 243

8. When you are close to incorporating as much chain as you want, use flush cutters to trim off the excess.

9. Continue working to secure the last few stones (figure 244).

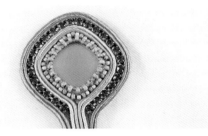

Figure 244

Chandelier crystals

Chandelier crystals come in a variety of sizes and shapes. Keep an eye out for the slightly smaller ones. Here's how to pocket a crystal.

1. After creating an element, determine the location from which you would like the crystal to protrude (figure 245).

Figure 245

2. Apply backing *but* do not apply any glue to the area where you are going to insert the crystal (figure 246). Allow the glue to dry completely.

Figure 246

3. Trim the backing. Note the unglued area now forms a flap of backing fabric (figure 247).

Figure 247

4. Starting just to the left of the open flap portion of the element, begin **edge beading** using the **brick stitch**. Continue edge beading all the way around the work until you reach the right side of the flap (figure 248). Remove the needle from the thread but leave the thread on the work.

Figure 248

5. Prepare the thread. (This is a new thread.)

6. Insert a crystal into the flap (figure 249).

Figure 249

7. Pull back the flap of synthetic suede and sew the crystal in place. When the thread exits the front of the work, make a **tacking stitch**, keeping it as small as possible so it doesn't show on the front of the work. Be sure the thread exits the back of the work to one side of the crystal, then sew down through the hole in the crystal so the thread exits front of work again (figure 250). Continue making tacking stitches over and through the hole of the crystal until there are three or four passes of thread wrapping each side of the top of the crystal (figure 251).

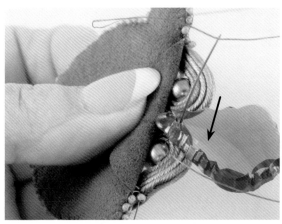

Figure 250

Figure 251

8. Carefully apply a thin layer of glue to the inside of the synthetic suede flap (figure 252). Position the flap over the crystal. While the glue is still wet, look at the work from the front and make sure the crystal is positioned as you wish (figure 253). Allow the glue to dry completely.

Figure 252

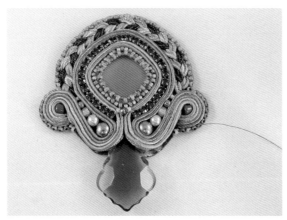

Figure 253

9. Rethread the needle with the thread you left trailing from the edge beading. Continue edge beading until you reach the point where the soutache work and the synthetic suede separate to accommodate the crystal (figure 254).

Figure 254

10. Picking up the edge of the synthetic suede only, edge bead behind the crystal (figure 255).

Figure 255

11. Where the synthetic suede and the front work rejoin on the other side of the crystal, begin edge beading again (figure 256). Complete the ring of edge beading and **bury the thread**.

Figure 256

12. Prepare the thread and **bury the knot** by sewing through a bead and the secured stack close to where the front work and synthetic suede separate to surround the crystal.

13. Picking up the front work only, edge bead across the front of the crystal (figure 257). When you reach the place where the front work and synthetic suede come back to together, bury the thread (figure 258).

Figure 257

Figure 258

Hoops

Metal and enameled hoops are a staple in jewelry fashion, and they are just as wonderful wrapped in soutache. Use metal hoops that have been soldered closed.

1. Prepare the thread.

2. Cut a length of soutache eight times longer than the diameter of your metal hoop. Put a dab of glue on the soutache 1 inch (2.5 cm) from the end

3. Lay the soldered seam of the hoop into the glue so the short end of the soutache is above the hoop (figure 259). Allow the glue to dry completely.

Figure 259

4. Hold the work gently. The glue is really only acting as an aid here; if you pull too hard on the soutache, it will pull off the hoop.

5. Pull the length of braid through the hoop. Wrap it over the hoop and pull it through again (figure 260).

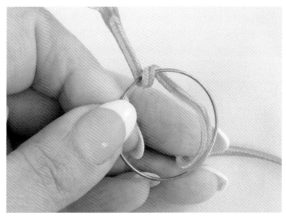

Figure 260

6. Continue working as in step 4. After you've completed a few wraps, you can grip the hoop by pinching the glued end of the soutache to keep it from coming free (figure 261).

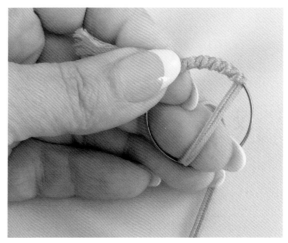

Figure 261

7. When you reach the glued end, one end of the soutache will lie flat over the other. Sew through the back layer of soutache from front to back (figure 262). Sew through both layers of soutache from back to front (figure 263). Retrace the thread path through both layers several times (figure 264).

Figure 262

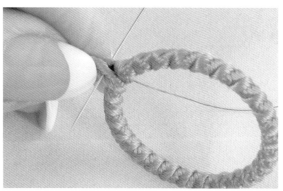

Figure 263

Figure 264

Note: The hoops can be wrapped in more than one color simply by laying two strands side by side at the gluing stage (figure 265). Work the same way as you did with the single strand, pulling the pair of strands through the hoop simultaneously (figure 266).

Figure 265

Figure 266

Twisted cord and braid. Often made of the same fibers and even available in the same dyes, twisted cord is a natural complement to soutache, adding an elegant texture. Can't find twisted cord in the color you want? Braid together a few strands of soutache and add a twist of your own.

Twisted Cord: Attaching to the outside of an element

　1. Prepare the thread.

2. Sew through the secured stack of a soutache shape so the thread exits the rib where you want your twisted cord to begin (figure 267).

Figure 267

3. Sew through the twisted cord about 1 inch (2.5 cm) from the cut end.

4. Make a tiny **tacking stitch** by sewing down through the twisted cord and into the secured stack (figure 268).

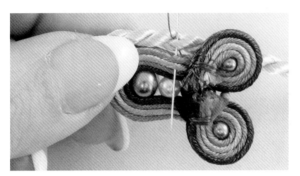

Figure 268

5. Working from right to left, repeat step 4 at ½-inch (1.3 cm) increments, securing the twisted cord around the shape (figure 269).

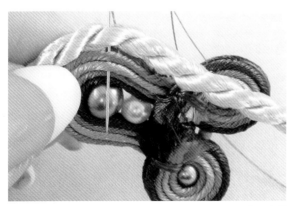

Figure 269

6. Following the directions for **ending a stack**, secure the twisted cord behind the work. Tack the cord behind the work, **whipstitch** through and over the cord, and cut off the excess (figure 270).

Figure 270

7. Pull the thread across the back of the work and following step 6, secure and trim the other end of the cord (figure 271).

Figure 271

Twisted cord can also be attached *inside* the stack and worked into almost any shape. This is just one example:

1. Cut four or more lengths of soutache.

2. Prepare the thread.

3. **Align and stack** the soutache and twisted cord so the soutache is at least two layers thick above and below the cord. Sew up through the center of the stack at the rib (figure 272).

Figure 272

4. Make a lollipop (figure 273).

Figure 273

Braided Soutache

1. Cut three lengths of soutache. Tie the ends together in an overhand knot. Separate the three strands (figure 274).

Figure 274

2. Bring the left strand over the center strand (figure 275).

Figure 275

3. Bring the right strand over the center strand (figure 276).

Figure 276

4. Repeat steps 2 and 3 until the braid is the length you want and tie the ends in an overhand knot (figure 277).

Figure 277

5. Following the directions for **Twisted Cord: Attaching to the Outside of an Element**, attach the braid to another element as desired (figure 278).

Figure 278

Backing and Edge Beading

Applying backing and **edge beading** (**brick stitch** style) are covered in this book in chapter 2. There are many different soutache and bead embroidery artists in the world, however, and—as in any art form—there is more than one way to do most things. In addition to explaining some of the various techniques you may encounter when looking at the work of other artists, this chapter will also give you some additional ideas for more embellished edge beading and edge-beading styles that can work well with chunkier pieces.

Backing

Glued backing. Using jewelry glue to apply a backing—whether it's synthetic suede, natural leather, or natural suede—is a common practice in the world of soutache and bead embroidery. While it has no mechanical connection, it offers the benefit of speed.

1. Use a ballpoint pen to trace the shape of your element onto the wrong side of the backing (figure 279).

Figure 279

2. Trim out the backing shape ¹⁄₁₆ to ⅛ inch (1.6 to 3 mm) *inside* the line (figure 280).

Figure 280

3. Put a medium-sized dollop of jewelry glue on the wrong side of the backing (figure 281) and use a toothpick to spread the glue thinly and evenly *all the way to the edges* (I recommend working on a piece of scrap paper when doing this) (figure 282).

Figure 281

Figure 282

4. Carefully position the backing over the back of the element and press it into place (figure 283). The backing should not be visible from the front of the work.

Figure 283

Glued and stitched backing. This method gives the clean (no edge bead) look preferred by some artists and provides the benefit of a mechanical bond, while eliminating the need for heavy jewelry glue.

1. Put a small amount of washable fabric glue on the back of the work (figure 284). Use your finger or a toothpick to spread it thinly.

Figure 284

2. Press the element on to the wrong side of the backing and allow the glue to dry completely.

3. Trim *as closely as possible to the work* (figure 285).

Figure 285

4. Bury the knot by sewing through a larger bead and out the back of the work near the edge of the backing (figure 286).

Figure 286

5. Pull the thread toward you over the edge of the backing and sew into the stack at the rib (figure 287). The needle should be angled upward and slightly to the right so the thread exits the back of the work close to the edge and to the right of where the thread last exited.

Figure 287

6. Working from left to right, continue following step 5 (figures 288 and 289).

Figure 288

Figure 289

Note: For this example, I intentionally used backing and thread that contrasts with the work so that it's easier to see. For this method in general, however, it's important to select backing and thread colors that blend as smoothly as possible with your soutache work.

Glued and edge-beaded backing. This is the method I use most often in my work. I feel that it gives the most finished look, the highest level of durability to the product, and the greatest number of design possibilities, particularly when it comes to connecting elements to one another. See **Apply backing** and **Edge beading** in chapter 2.

Inner stabilizers. Some people feel the back of soutache and bead embroidery is a little lumpy for their liking. Personally, I find if I use a smaller amount of washable fabric glue, the **edge-beading** process actually lifts and stretches the backing across the back of the work, minimizing any lumps. If you want a super-smooth back side, however, try using an inner stabilizer.

1. Trace your soutache shape onto a piece of card stock (figure 290).

Figure 290

2. Sketch a line approximately ⅛ to 3⁄16 inch (3 to 5 mm) inside the traced line.

3. Cut on the inner line (figure 291).

Figure 291

4. Test-fit the card stock on the back of the work—be sure a thin margin of the work is visible beyond the card stock all the way around (figure 292).

Figure 292

5. Apply a small amount of washable fabric glue to work side of the card stock (the "front" or the face of the card stock that will be touching the soutache work) and spread it thinly.

6. Lay the card stock glue side down on the back of the work (figure 293). Allow the glue to dry completely.

Figure 293

7. Apply a small amount of washable fabric glue to the back of the work (including the card stock) (figure 294) and spread it thinly.

Figure 294

8. Lay the work glue side down onto wrong side of the backing (figure 295). Allow the glue to dry completely.

Figure 295

9. Trim the backing and **edge bead** as desired.

Setting a curve

When creating a soft cuff, making the entire bracelet flat and then bending it around your wrist is guaranteed to result in kinks and wrinkles. Use the following method to make smooth, round cuffs.

1. Apply washable fabric glue to the back of the work. Spread it thinly, making sure all threads are coated with glue (figure 296).

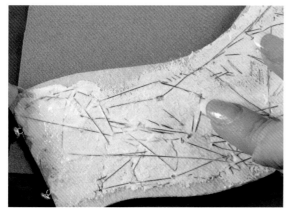

Figure 296

2. Lay the work glue side down onto the wrong side of the backing

3. While the glue is still wet, wrap the work over a 10-ounce soup can. Tug the backing gently to stretch and remove any wrinkles (figure 297).

Figure 297

4. Secure the work by tying an extra piece of soutache around the work and the can (figure 298). (There's no need to tie it tightly—you don't want to leave indents in the front of your work.) Allow the glue to dry completely.

Figure 298

Edge Beading Styles

Smooth edge. If you are creating an element that does not need fringe or sewn connections, you might try a smooth edge finish. If you look carefully, you'll see the only change between this and the **brick stitch** edge-beading technique is the direction you sew through the bead when you go into it the second time. The finished look, however, is very different because the beads now sit with their holes running parallel to the work (beads run hole to hole) instead of perpendicular (holes up).

1. Prepare the thread and **bury the knot** by sewing though one of the larger beads in the work and through the stack so the thread exits the outer edge of the work at the rib (figure 299).

Figure 299

2. Holding the work facedown, pick up two 11° seed beads. Working from left to right, sew into the rib two bead widths away from where the thread last exited. Insert the needle at an upward angle so the thread exits the backing near the edge (figure 300).

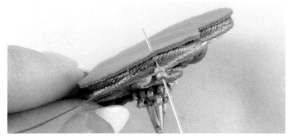

Figure 300

3. Pull the thread over the edge of the work and sew through the left hole of the right bead (the needle should be entering between the first and second bead) (figure 301).

Figure 301

4. Pick up an 11° seed bead. Working from left to right, sew into the rib one bead width away from where the thread last exited (figure 302).

Figure 302

5. Pull the thread over the edge of the work and sew through the left hole of rightmost bead (the needle should be entering between the second-to-last and last beads) (figure 303).

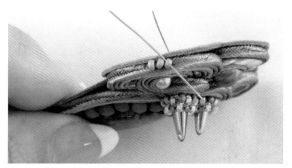

Figure 303

6. Continue following steps 4 and 5. Notice how the beads line up hole to hole (figure 304).

Figure 304

7. After adding the last bead, complete the pattern by sewing through the first bead and the rib, and out the backing. **Bury the thread** (figure 305).

Figure 305

Brick stitch edge. See **Brick stitch** in chapter 2 (figure 306).

Figure 306

Decorated edges

If you finish your work with **brick stitch edge beading**, there are numerous ways to add decorative touches either by adding beads during the **edge-beading** process, such as in picot edges, or by coming back and adding embellishments later.

Picot

1. Follow the directions for **brick stitch**, but before picking up a new 11° seed bead, pick up a 15° seed bead (figure 307).

Figure 307

2. Just as you would in standard **brick stitch edge beading**, sew into the work at the rib one bead width away from where the thread last exited (figure 308).

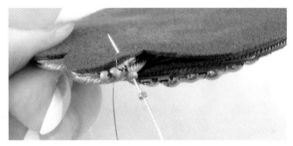

Figure 308

3. Pull the thread over the edge of the work. Sew through the right hole of rightmost bead. The 15° seed bead will sit up on top of the two 11° seed beads (figure 309).

Figure 309

4. Continue following the directions for brick stitch edge beading, adding picots wherever you want them.

Note: In this example, I added a picot between every other pair of 11° seed beads (figure 310), but you can add one between every pair or in any other pattern you find pleasing.

Figure 310

Embellished Edges

1. After completing **brick stitch edge beading**, **bury the knot** by sewing into one of the beads on the front of the work, into the work, and out one of the edge beads (figure 311).

Figure 311

2. Pick up an 11° seed bead, an 8°, and a 15° seed bead (figure 312).

Figure 312

3. Sew back through the 8° seed bead (leaving the 15° seed bead to act as a stop bead) and pick up an 11° seed bead (figure 313).

Figure 313

4. Sew into the edge bead adjacent to the one the thread last exited (figure 314).

Figure 314

5. Sew up through the next edge bead (figure 315).

Figure 315

6. Continue following steps 2 through 5 (figure 316).

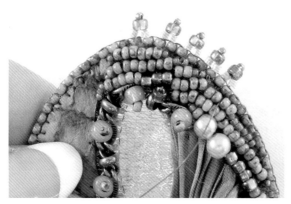

Figure 316

Note: You can easily change the look of this embellishment by changing bead sizes (figure 317). If you change from 11° seed beads to a larger size, however, you may need to skip over an edge bead before sewing back down into the work to allow adequate space (figure 318).

Figure 317

Figure 318

Fringe

There are two differences between fringe and other forms of beaded-edge embellishment: the length of the run of beads added, and sewing back into the same edge bead. Thread tension is important here. On one hand, you want to keep it snug enough that no thread is exposed in your individual fringes. On the other hand, do not make it so tight that the fringes stiffen—you want them to swing freely.

1. After completing **brick stitch edge beading, bury the knot** by sewing into one of the beads on the front of the work and into the work.

2. Sew out through the first edge bead you would like to embellish with fringe (figure 319).

Figure 319

3. Pick up a run of beads. Select any beads you like, but fringe will usually hang more consistently if you end each strand of fringe with a slightly larger bead than the ones used in the overall length. Then add a 15° or 11° seed bead to act as a stop bead.

4. Sew back through all the beads in the strand except the stop bead (figure 320).

Figure 320

5. Sew into the same edge bead from which the strand originated (figure 321).

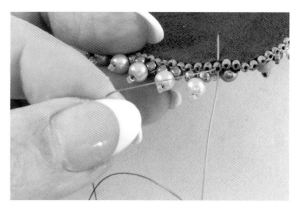

Figure 321

Note: Sewing through the very edge of the backing at this stage is a good way to help reinforce the fringe.

6. Sew through the next edge bead you want to embellish with fringe (figure 322).

Figure 322

7. Continue following steps 3 through 6 as desired.

Note: Fringe strands can all be the same length, or they can be graduated from short to long and back again. They can be made so the beads are the same in each strand, or you can change bead styles, colors, and sizes to create variations and texture (figure 323).

Figure 323

Negative spaces

The smallest negative spaces (the "holes" or "empty spaces" in the soutache work) can usually be left alone with the backing showing through. Larger negative spaces, however, are a nice opportunity for adding airiness to your work.

1. Press a darning needle through the backing behind the negative space, leaving a small hole (figure 324).

Figure 324

2. Using very small scissors, make pairs of small snips from the hole toward the nearby stacks, creating tiny triangular flaps (figure 325).

Figure 325

3. Working from the back, snip away the small, triangular bits of backing. Work slowly and carefully, enlarging the hole little by little so as not to damage the soutache (figure 326).

Figure 326

4. Prepare the thread. Bury the knot by sewing into one of the larger beads and out of the stack surrounding the negative space at the rib (figure 327).

Figure 327

5. Bring the thread toward you through the negative space (figure 328).

Figure 328

6. Following the directions for **brick stitch edge beading**, pick up two seed beads (depending on the size of the negative space, use 11° or 15° seed beads) (figure 329).

Figure 329

7. Working from left to right, sew into the stack at the rib so the thread exits the synthetic suede on the back of the work (figure 330).

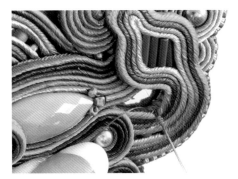

Figure 330

8. Pulling the thread toward you over the edge of the backing, sew through the right hole of rightmost bead (figure 331), bringing thread back through the negative space.

Figure 331

9. Pick up another bead and continue on as in **brick stitch edge beading** understanding that in order to get your needle angled properly, you will most likely have to pass your thread back and forth through the negative space (figure 332).

Figure 332

Zipper edge

For chunkier projects, a zipper edge gives a more proportional finish.

1. Prepare the thread and **bury the knot** by sewing through one of the larger beads in the design and out the stack at the rib (figure 333).

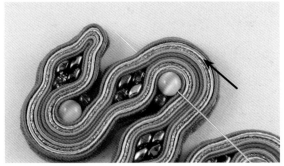

Figure 333

2. Holding the work facedown, sew back into a rib very close to where the thread exited it. Sew on an upward angle so the thread exits the backing close to the edge (figure 334).

Figure 334

3. Pull the thread toward you over the edge of the work. Pick up two 11° seed beads. Sew into the rib on an upward angle so the thread exits the backing one bead width away from where the thread last exited the backing (figure 335).

Figure 335

4. Sew through the bead closest to the backing so the thread exits between the two beads (figure 336).

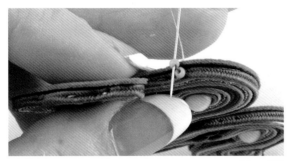

Figure 336

5. Pick up two more 11° seed beads. Sew into the rib one bead width away from where the thread last entered the stack. Sew on an upward angle so the thread exits one bead width away from where thread last exited the backing (figure 337).

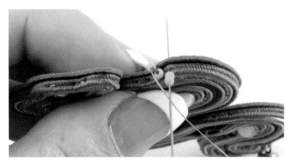

Figure 337

6. Of the two beads most recently added, sew through the bead closest to the backing so the thread exits between the last two beads added (figure 338).

Figure 338

7. Continue following steps 5 and 6. The resulting pattern—with half the beads sitting hole side down on the stack and half the beads standing on edge behind the first half—looks a bit like a garment zipper (figure 339).

Figure 339

8. After the last two beads have been added, complete the pattern by sewing through the first two beads, into the stack, and out the backing. **Bury the thread.**

Rope edge

This is an excellent choice for projects comprised of multiple layers resulting in thicker edges.

1. Prepare the thread and **bury the knot** by sewing through one of the beads in the design and out the backing close to the edge (figure 340).

Figure 340

2. Pull the thread toward you over the edge of the work. Pick up three 11° seed beads. Sew into the front of the work on an upward angle so the thread exits the backing one bead width away from where the thread last exited the backing (figure 341).

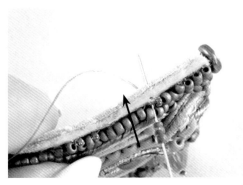

Figure 341

3. Sew through the bead closest to the backing so the thread exits between that bead and the middle bead in the run (figure 342).

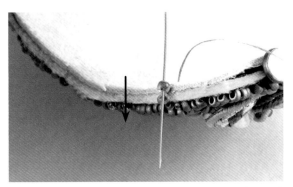

Figure 342

4. Pick up three more 11° seed beads. Sew into the front of the work one bead width away from where the thread last entered. Sew on an upward angle so the thread exits one bead width away from where the thread last exited the backing (figure 343).

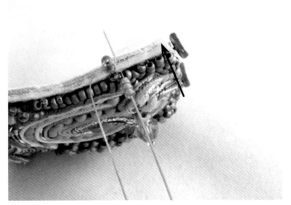

Figure 343

5. Of the three beads most recently added, sew through the bead closest to the backing so the thread exits between that bead and the middle bead in the run (figure 344).

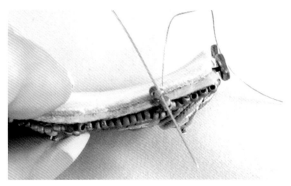

Figure 344

6. Continue following steps 4 and 5. The resulting pattern has the appearance of twisted rope (figure 345).

Figure 345

7. After the last three beads have been added, complete the pattern by sewing through the first three beads, into the work, and out the backing. **Bury the thread.**

Note: I've done this example in three different colors of beads to make it easier to see the pattern, but you can use as many or few colors as you like.

Attachment Techniques

While it is possible to make an entire piece of jewelry starting with one very long stack and simply working it to the ends (and that can be a super-fun challenge!), most pieces are made with multiple smaller pieces that are connected in various ways. Being familiar with the different attachment techniques will encourage greater creativity in your work and will allow you to work more efficiently. Because smaller components feel less "precious," we're not so afraid of messing them up and we may work on them with greater confidence.

Beaded/sewn connections

One of the most common (and easiest) ways to connect elements relies on the components having **brick stitch edge beading** so these connections are built *after* the components are **backed** and **edge beaded**.

1. Lay your components out in the arrangement you want (figure 346).

Figure 346

2. Take a few moments to consider where the best places for attachment might be. (I recommend having at least two connections between components, otherwise they may flip or spin when worn.)

3. Prepare the thread and **bury the knot** by sewing through one of the larger beads in the component and sewing out through the **edge beading** at the desired attachment point (figure 347).

Figure 347

4. Pick up the beads for your connection (in my example, I've used an 11°, 8°, and 11° seed bead, but you can use whatever you like). Remember that short connections help finished work look more solid, while longer connections will give the work more airiness.

5. Sew into the second component. I recommend you sew through the backing near the edge as this will add strength to the connection (figure 348).

Figure 348

6. Retrace the thread path back through the backing and the edge beading of the second component, the connection, and the edge beading and backing of the first component (figure 349).

Figure 349

7. Work your way over to the second connection location by **surface diving** underneath the backing (figure 350).

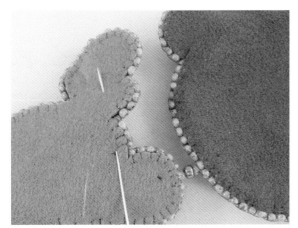

Figure 350

8. Following steps 4 through 6, make your second connection (figure 351). **Bury the thread.**

Figure 351

9. Continue to make connections as needed (figure 352).

Figure 352

Continuous ladder connections. Make two smaller components look like they were made as one. These connections are done *before* **backing** and **edge beading**.

1. Consider the way you would like two components to connect to one another (figure 353). This works best when two convex or prominent areas are pointing toward one another.

Figure 353

2. Prepare the thread. Sew into the back of the work so the thread exits the outer stack at the rib close to where the curve meets the rest of the component (figure 354).

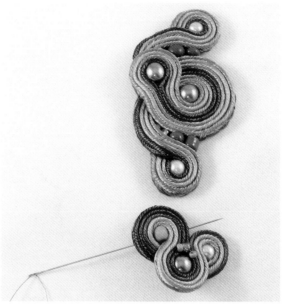

Figure 354

3. Pick up a bead (I've selected an 8° seed bead, but you should choose a bead that is proportional to the components and stacks you are working with). Cut three or four lengths of soutache, each 2 inches (5.1 cm) longer than the length of the ladder you are creating. Align and stack the lengths. Sew through the new stack about 1 inch (2.5 cm) from the end (figure 355).

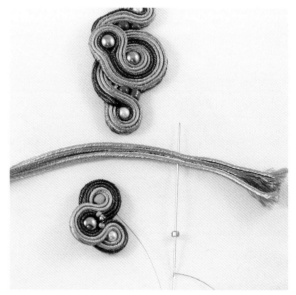

Figure 355

4. Following the directions for ladders, create a ladder that wraps approximately halfway around the prominent area of the component (figure 356).

Figure 356

5. Set the stitch by **retracing the thread path** one or two times through the secured stack, bead, and the working stack (figure 357).

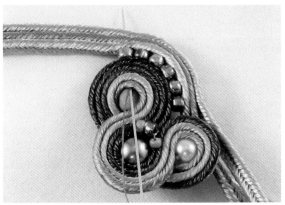

Figure 357

6. Pick up a bead and sew through the secured stack of the second component at the point you would like to begin surrounding it with the rest of the ladder (figure 358).

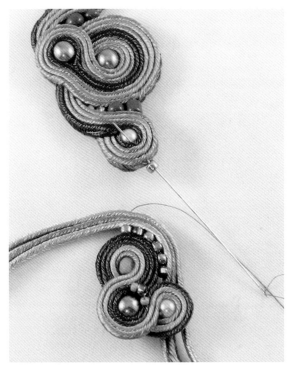

Figure 358

7. Following the directions for ladders, create a ladder that wraps halfway around the prominent area of the second component (figure 359).

Figure 359

8. End the stack. Prepare the thread and sew back into the work near the beginning of the ladder. End the stack (figure 360).

Figure 360

Kissing connections

Components can be connected simply by laying the edge of one stack against another and stitching them together. This works particularly well with identical or mirrored components. These are done *before* **backing** and **edge beading**.

1. Determine where you want two components to connect (figure 361).

Figure 361

2. Prepare the thread. On back of the work, **bury the knot** or simply sew into the back of the stack close to where you want the connection.

3. Sew through both components at the connection point (figure 362).

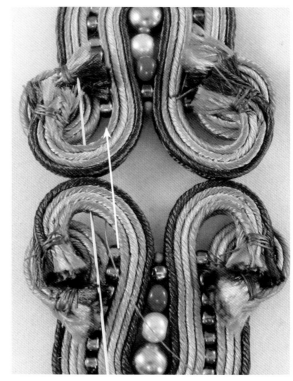

Figure 362

4. Reinforce the connection by **retracing the thread path** as needed.

5. Either by **tracing a path** or **surface diving,** work your way across the back of the work to the next connection point (figure 363) and work as in steps 3 and 4 (figure 364).

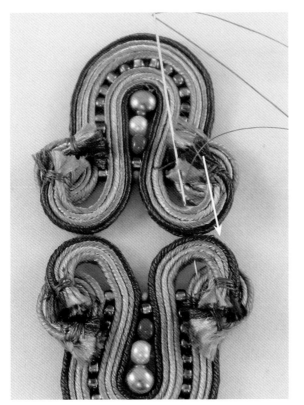

Figure 363

6. End the thread (figure 365).

Figure 365

Figure 364

Layered connections

Simple layered connections

Remember all those lollipops you made out of your scraps? Grab them and turn a simple component into an explosion of colors and shapes (figure 366). These are done *before* **backing** and **edge beading**.

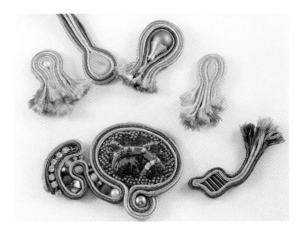

Figure 366

1. Prepare the thread.

2. Position a lollipop behind the work (figure 367).

Figure 367

3. Secure the lollipop with **tacking stitches** (figure 368). (I recommend using three or four tacking stitches for each component added).

Figure 368

4. Following steps 2 and 3, add more components as desired (figure 369).

Figure 369

Layered and wrapped connections

These connections can give otherwise flat work a look of undulating movement.

1. Select a small component that ends with a longer stack that can act like a stem. Following the directions for Simple Layered Connections (page 101), **tack** the component behind the work at the desired location (figure 370).

Figure 370

2. Bend the "stem" over and around the edge of the larger component and tack in place (figure 371).

Figure 371

Note: If you make two small components with identical stack colors and orders, you can make layered and wrapped connections that give the illusion of being continuous—the eye assumes they connect in the back, even though it would impossible to make a component with no cut ends (figures 372 and 373). If the end of a component happens to land on a smooth surface like a large bead or cabochon, put a dab of glue under the component (figure 374).

Figure 372

Figure 373

Figure 374

Pivoting/articulating connections

These are made *in between* **backed** and **edge-beaded** components. The finished work drapes beautifully.

Method #1: Staged connections

These connections are made by making the connection and *then* **backing** and **edge beading** the lower component alternately. This process is a little fussier than **Method #2**, but there are no stitches showing on the back of the components when you're done.

1. Apply backing and edge bead the component you want to be the top layer (figure 375).

Figure 375

2. Prepare the thread. Sew up through the component you want to be the bottom layer at desired pivot point (figure 376).

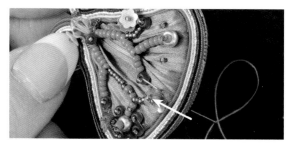

Figure 376

3. Pick up a 4 mm bead.

4. Sew up through upper component at the pivot point desired (figure 377).

Figure 377

5. Following directions for **tacking stitches**, sew down through the *upper* component, bead, and lower component (figure 378). **Retrace the thread path** to reinforce the connection as needed.

Figure 378

6. Take a few **shallow stitches** on the back of the lower component (figure 379). Trim the thread.

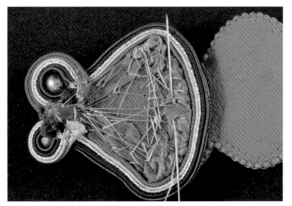

Figure 379

7. Apply backing and edge bead the lower component (figure 380).

Figure 380

8. Select another unbacked component to be the new bottom component. The former bottom component will become the top component in the pair. Follow steps 3 through 7. Repeat until your work has reached the desired length (figure 381).

Figure 381

Method #2

This is the faster, easier method for making **pivoting/articulating connections**, and if you keep the **tacking stitches** very small, they will sink into the synthetic suede and be virtually invisible.

1. Prepare the thread. Sew down through the lower component at the attachment area (figure 382).

Figure 382

2. Making the smallest possible tacking stitch on the face of the backing, **retrace the thread path** (figure 383). Pick up a bead (the example is using a 4 mm glass pearl).

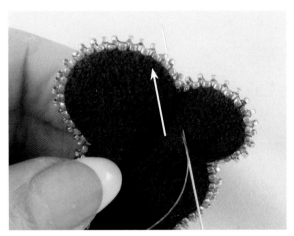

Figure 383

3. Sew up through the upper component at the attachment point (figure 384). Retrace the thread path through the upper component, bead, and lower component three times (figure 385). **Bury the thread.** Snip the thread.

Figure 384

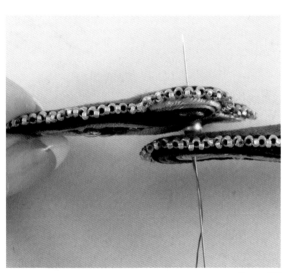

Figure 385

Finely Finished

When you first start working in soutache and bead embroidery, there's a lot of focus on—well—the focal pieces. When you're done making a pendant or a bracelet center, you're probably so excited about it that you just want to attach it to a piece of manufactured chain or a length of ribbon and wear it to the grocery store. And there's nothing wrong with that—sometimes "quick and simple" is all that's required. But with a tiny little bit more work and some imagination, you can implement finishing techniques that will elevate your work from "finally done" to "finely finished"!

Bands and Swags

Bands

Chain stitch is a technique that is especially useful for making bands for necklaces and bracelets.

1. Prepare the thread.

2. Cut three lengths of soutache, each one twice as long as you want your band to be, plus 6 inches (15.2 cm).

3. Fold over the end of one length of soutache and slide a jump ring onto the strand (figure 386).

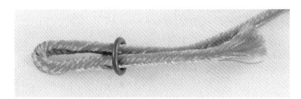

Figure 386

4. Move the jump ring to the middle of the strand. **Align and stack** the remaining two lengths under the first one. Sew up through the stack at the rib just right of center (figure 387).

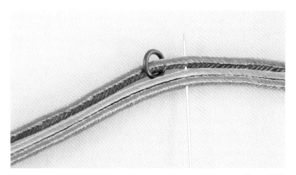

Figure 387

5. Working from right to left, pass the needle through the jump ring.

6. Sew down through stack, capturing the jump ring with a stitch (figure 388).

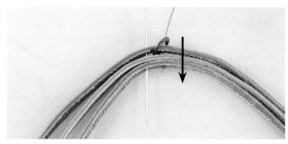

Figure 388

7. Pick up a 4 mm bead and sew across through the right-hand stack. Work in **chain stitch** until your band is ½ inch (1.3 cm) shorter than your desired band length. **Split** the stack symmetrically (figure 389).

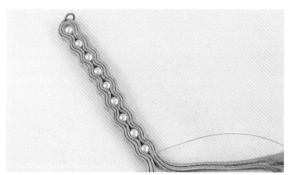

Figure 389

8. Pick up a 6 mm bead and **end the stack**. Pull the thread across the back of the work and sew into the work so the thread exits the other side of the join. Pick up a 4 mm bead and end the stack (figure 390).

Figure 390

9. With washable fabric glue, **apply backing** only to the area of the band where you ended the stacks (figure 391). Allow the glue to dry completely.

Figure 391

10. Trim the backing (figure 392). Where the backing passes behind the unbacked area of the band, trim the backing into a smooth curve (figure 393).

Figure 392

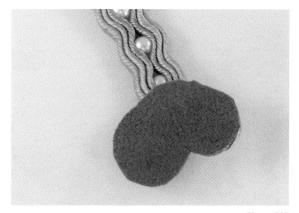

Figure 393

11. Edge bead using the **brick stitch edge** beading technique (figure 394).

Figure 394

12. Attach the band to the work as in **Beaded/Sewn Connections** (figure 395).

Figure 395

13. Following steps 1 through 12, make a **mirror** image of the first band and attach it to the work (figure 396).

Figure 396

Knotting and gnarling

Create highly textural bands to show off chunky or more organic pieces.

1. Prepare the thread.

2. Cut as many lengths of soutache as you want in your band, each one four times longer than the desired length of the band.

3. Fold over the end of one length and slip a jump ring onto the strand (figure 397).

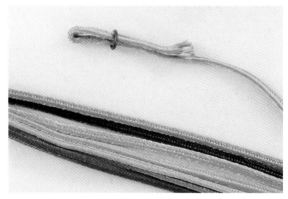

Figure 397

4. Slide the jump ring to the center of the strand (figure 398).

Figure 398

5. Align and stack all the strands. Insert the needle through the center of the stack at the rib (figure 399). *Do not pull the thread through—you're just using the needle as a placeholder.*

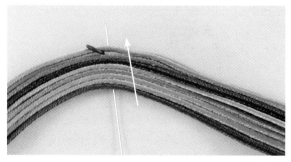

Figure 399

6. Cross one end of the stack over the other and make an overhand knot, keeping the jump ring centered at the top of the knot. Pull the knot tight and remove the needle (figure 400).

Figure 400

7. Unravel the end of one strand by dragging the tip of a darning needle through the rib (figure 401).

Figure 401

8. Carefully pull apart the fine wrapping fibers until the slightly thicker core fibers are exposed (figure 402).

Figure 402

9. Grasp one of the core fibers. Grip the soutache just above the place you want a gnarl to appear (figure 403). Pull the core fiber and a gnarl will appear below the point you were grasping the braid (figure 404).

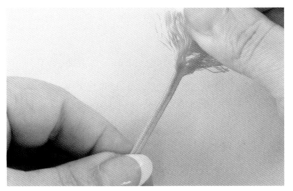

Figure 403

Figure 404

10. Following steps 7 through 9, unravel and add a gnarl to each strand (figure 405).

Figure 405

11. Pinch together two of the strands so their ends align. Sew through them approximately 1½ inches (3.8 cm) from their ends (figure 406).

Figure 406

12. Continue adding strands to the stack, sewing through each until all the strands are gathered up (figure 407). Reinforce by **retracing the thread path** through the stack two or three times (figure 408).

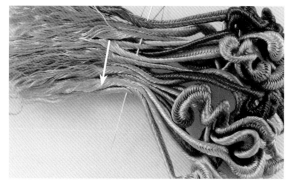

Figure 407

Figure 408

13. Begin wrapping the thread tightly around the stack (figure 409). Occasionally sew through the stack to secure the thread. Continue wrapping and securing thread until there is a band of thread approximately ¼ inch (6 mm) wide (figure 410).

Figure 409

Figure 410

14. Trim off the ends of the soutache (figure 411).

Figure 411

15. Work as in **Apply End Caps** (figure 412).

Figure 412

16. Attach knotted and gnarled bands to work with the bead-chain links (figure 413).

Figure 413

Note: I used short lengths of soutache for this example, resulting in cute little "poofs," but you can use much longer strands and add multiple gnarls on each strand (figure 414).

Figure 414

Swags

Beaded/sewn connections are described in **Attachment Techniques**. But strung beads can be used for more than simply attaching one component to another. Consider stringing multiple strands of graduating lengths between components to create a decorative swag that can become just as important an element to the finished work as the soutache components. This is an excellent place to incorporate beads that—due to their shape, size, or translucency—may not work as well within the soutache (figure 415).

Figure 415

Chain and bead chain can also be used to make swags, but it takes some planning because you need to add jump rings at the connection points (figure 416).

Figure 416

Endings

Kumihimo end caps

Apply end caps

1. Put a small amount of cyanoacrylate jewelry gel glue inside the kumihimo end cap (figure 417).

Figure 417

2. Press an end cap over the cut end of braid (figure 418).

Figure 418

Net end caps. While you can glue your end caps on and leave it at that, you *know* I'm a stickler about having a mechanical bond in addition to an adhesive one. Here's a technique that provides greater security and disguises the end caps.

1. Prepare the thread. Sew through the braid just under the end cap (figure 419).

Figure 419

2. Pick up eighteen beads in a pattern of two 11° seed beads and one 8° seed bead (figure 420).

Figure 420

Note: The goal here is to wrap the braid in a regularly patterned ring of beads. Depending on the type of braid you used, how tightly you made your kumihimo, and the beads you select, you may end up with a pattern of six sets of three beads or five sets of four beads—play with it a bit and find the best fit.

3. Wrap a strand of beads around the braid and sew through the first set of beads in the ring (figure 421).

Figure 421

4. Secure the ring position by sewing through the braid and back through the beads in a couple of places (figure 422).

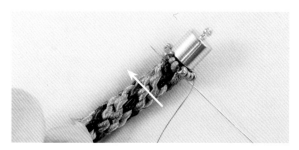

Figure 422

5. Sew through one of the larger beads (figure 423).

Figure 423

6. Pick up five beads in a pattern of two 11°s, one 8°, and two 11° seed beads (figure 424).

Figure 424

7. Sew through the next 8° seed bead in the ring (figure 425).

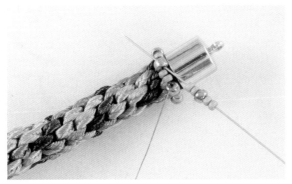

Figure 425

8. Repeat steps 6 and 7 until you sew through the first 8° seed bead in the ring. (You should have one loop of five beads for each 8° seed bead in the ring.)

9. Step up by sewing through the first three beads in the first loop (the thread should be exiting the 8° seed bead at the center of the loop) (figure 426).

Figure 426

10. Pick up five beads in a pattern of two 11°s, one 8°, and two 11° seed beads.

11. Sew through the 8° seed bead in the next loop (figure 427).

Figure 427

12. Repeat steps 10 and 11 until you sew through the 8° seed bead in the first loop. (This completes a second ring of loops.)

13. Step up by sewing through the first three beads in the first loop of the second ring of loops. Work as in steps 10 through 12, creating a third ring of loops (figure 428).

Figure 428

14. Step up by sewing through the first three beads in the first loop of the third ring of loops (thread should be exiting the 8° at the center of the loop) (figure 429).

Figure 429

15. Pick up two 11° seed beads (figure 430). Sew through the 8° seed bead in the next loop (figure 431).

Figure 430

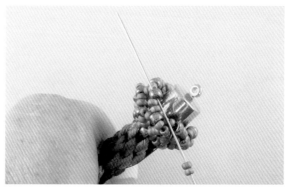

Figure 431

16. Repeat step 15 until you sew through the first 8° seed bead in the ring. Sew through this top ring of beads two or three times, increasing thread tension while pushing the net of beads up the cylinder of the end cap until the top ring of beads closes over the end of the cap (figure 432).

Figure 432

17. Trace a path back through the beads of the netting until you reach the braid. Sew through the braid several times to secure the thread and trim (figure 433).

Figure 433

18. Repeat on other end cap.

19. Add a **bead chain** and a toggle to make up the 3 inches (7.6 cm) subtracted in step 10 of **Make a Braid**.

Open Netting

1. Prepare the thread.

2. Sew through the soutache-wrapped joint near the end of the coil (figure 434).

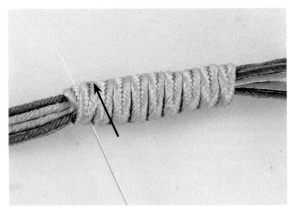

Figure 434

3. Pick up 15 beads in a pattern of two 11° seed beads and one 8° seed bead.

Note: The goal here is to wrap the coil in a regularly patterned ring of beads. Depending on the type of braid you used, how tightly you made your coil, and the beads you select, you may end up with a pattern of five sets of three beads or four sets of four beads—play with it a bit to find the best fit.

4. Wrap the strand of beads around the base of the coil and sew through the first set of beads in the ring (figure 435).

Figure 435

5. Secure the ring position by sewing through the coil and back through the beads in a couple of places (figure 436).

Figure 436

6. Sew through one of the larger beads (figure 437).

Figure 437

7. Pick up five beads in a pattern of two 11°, one 8°, and two 11° seed beads.

8. Sew through the next 8° seed bead in the ring (figure 438).

Figure 438

9. Repeat steps 7 and 8 until you sew through the first 8° seed bead bead in the ring (figure 439). (You should have one loop of five beads for each 8° seed bead in the ring—this completes the first ring of loops.)

Figure 439

10. Step up by sewing through the first three beads in the first loop (the thread should be exiting the 8° seed bead at the center of the loop) (figure 440).

Figure 440

11. Pick up five beads in a pattern of two 11°, one 8°, and two 11° seed beads. Sew through the 8° seed bead in the next loop of the first ring of loops (figure 441). This begins a second ring of loops.

Figure 441

12. Repeat step 11 until you sew through the 8° seed bead in the first loop in the first ring of loops. (This completes a second ring of loops.)

13. Continue following steps 10 through 12, periodically sewing down into the coil to stabilize the netting and hold it in place (figure 442).

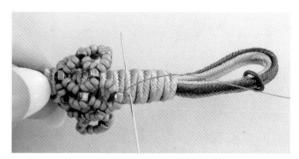

Figure 442

14. When you have covered as much of the coil as you want, step up and add two 11° seed beads between each of the 8° seed beads in the last ring of loops (figure 443).

Figure 443

15. Sew through the last ring once or twice, adding enough thread tension to tighten the ring. Sew through the coil four or five times to secure the thread (figure 444). Trim the thread.

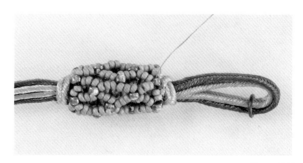

Figure 444

PART 2

THE
PROJECTS

Tripping the Light Fantastic Earrings

En-LIGHT-en yourself about the possibilities of soutache and bead embroidery. Rather than standard lollipops, the splashes on the bottoms of these earrings are designed to allow light to pass through the bicone crystals.

MATERIALS & TOOLS

Beads

2 turquoise 12 x 18 mm flat faceted teardrop shaped beads

4 lavender 6 mm AB bicone crystals

2 gray-blue 6 mm AB bicone crystals

1 g silver 8° seed beads

1 g silver-lined blue 11° seed beads

1 g purple-lined clear 11° matte seed beads

4 silver 4 mm glass pearls

Soutache

1 yard (91.4 cm) each of BeadSmith brand ⅛-inch (3 mm) soutache in the following colors:

    mint

    textured rainbow metallic

    blue

    smog

    smog/linen stripe

    lavender

4 ½ x 3-inch (11.4 x 7.6 cm) piece of powder blue Nicole's BeadBacking beading foundation

Cathy blue size B Nymo beading thread

6 inches (15.2 cm) of gold crystal AB rhinestone chain (6.5 SS [stone size])

2 gold 6 mm soldered jump rings

4 ½ x 3-inch (11.4 x 7.6 cm) piece of gray synthetic suede

Pair of gold earwires

Washable fiber glue

Scissors

Size 10 beading needle

Flat-nose or chain-nose pliers

SKILLS USED

Large Beads (page 55)

Embellishing with Backstitch 2 (page 63)

Working off the Beading Foundation (page 63)

Adding Soutache around Beading Foundation (page 65)

Steps

Prepare the focal beads

1. Cut the piece of beading foundation in half. Put a small dab of glue in the center of each piece. Place a flat faceted teardrop shaped bead in the glue on each piece and set them aside to dry completely (figure 1).

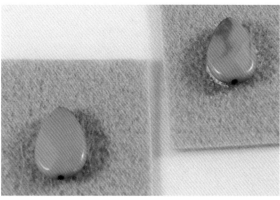

Figure 1

Make splashes

1. Prepare the thread.

2. Cut three 4-inch (10.2 cm) lengths of soutache—one each of mint, textured rainbow metallic, and blue. **Align and stack** them in that order from bottom to top. Sew up through the center of the stack, keeping the needle in the ribs (figure 2).

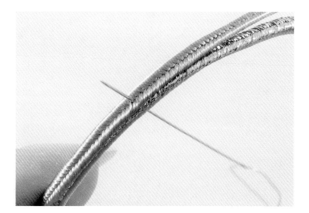

Figure 2

3. Working from right to left, make one **shaping stitch** about ⅜ inch (9.5 mm) long (figure 3).

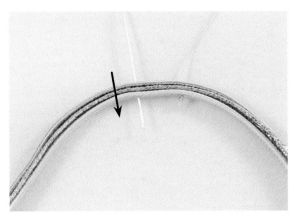

Figure 3

4. Pick up one lavender 6 mm bicone crystal. Sew up through the stack very close to the knot (figure 4).

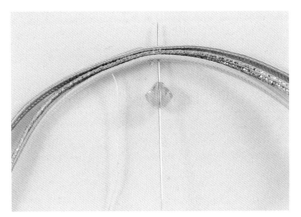

Figure 4

5. Turn the work 90° to the right so the hole of the crystal runs horizontally and the stack is now wrapping over the new top of the crystal. **Retrace the thread path** through the stack, crystal, and stack (figure 5).

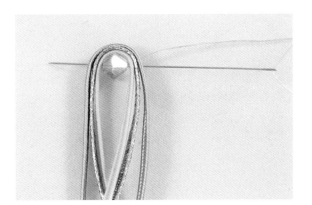

Figure 5

6. Working from top to bottom, make one **shaping stitch** about ⅜ inch (9.5 mm) long. Sew through the stack directly across from where the thread exits (figure 6). **Retrace the thread path twice.**

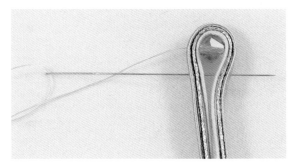

Figure 6

7. Working from top to bottom, consolidate the large stack with two **shaping stitches** (figure 7). **Set the last stitch** by **retracing the thread path**. Trim the thread.

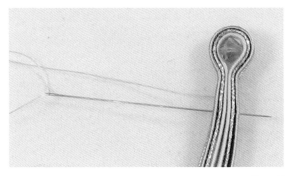

Figure 7

8. Repeat steps 1 through 7 using a gray-blue bicone. Repeat steps 1 through 7 with a lavender bicone (figure 8).

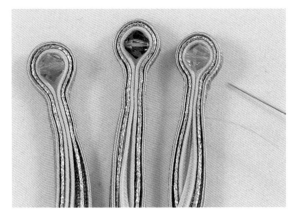

Figure 8

Tripping the Light Fantastic Earrings **121**

9. Place the second lavender component to the right of the gray-blue component. Sew through both large stacks (figure 9).

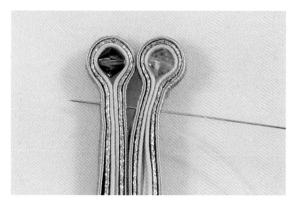

Figure 9

10. Retrace the thread path four times, adding a slight amount of thread tension with each pass to pull the components into the desired shape (figure 10).

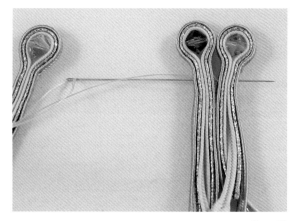

Figure 10

11. Sew through the third element. Sewing through the combined stacks of all three elements, work as in step 10 to complete the splash shape (figure 11). Trim the thread.

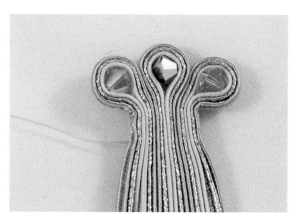

Figure 11

12. Trim the extra soutache from the splash approximately ½ inch (1.3 cm) from the crystals (figure 12).

Figure 12

13. Repeat steps 1 through 12 for the second earring.

Center the element

1. Prepare a new thread. Sew up through the beading foundation very close to the flat faceted teardrop shaped bead. Following the directions for **Large Beads**, secure the flat faceted teardrop shaped bead to the beading foundation (figure 13).

Figure 13

2. Using 8° seed beads and following the directions for **Embellishing with Backstitch 2**, surround the flat faceted teardrop shaped bead with a row of backstitch 2 (figure 14). Sew up through the beading foundation very close to the flat faceted teardrop shaped bead. Pick up two 8° seed beads.

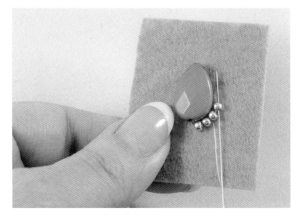

Figure 14

3. Sew through the entire ring of beads to smooth the curve and help fill gaps (figure 15).

Figure 16

Figure 15

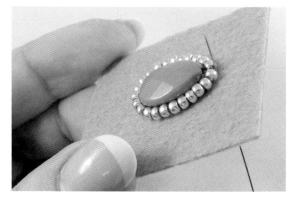

Figure 17

5. Sew up through the beading foundation just outside the 8° seed beads near the point of the flat faceted teardrop shaped bead (figure 18).

4. Sew down through the beading foundation between the flat faceted teardrop shaped bead and the 8° seed beads (figure 16). Secure the thread by making a couple of **shallow stitches** behind the work (figure 17).

Figure 18

6. Drape the rhinestone chain around the work so the first stone is placed near point of the flat faceted teardrop shaped bead (figure 19). Following the directions for **Working off the Beading Foundation**, secure the chain around the beads (figure 20).

Figure 19

Figure 20

7. Trim the beading foundation away from work. *Do not overtrim.* Leave a 1 mm margin of beading foundation visible from the front of the work (figure 21).

Figure 21

8. Sew into the back of the beading foundation so the thread exits the very edge of the beading foundation at the bottom center of the teardrop shape (figure 22).

Figure 22

9. Cut three 8-inch (20.3 cm) lengths of soutache: one smog, smog/linen stripe, and one lavender. Locate the center of the smog length and sew through the soutache at the rib (figure 23).

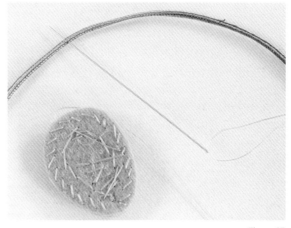

Figure 23

10. Following the directions for **Adding Soutache around Beading Foundation**, attach the smog piece of soutache around the foundation and then the stack of two, with the stripe on the bottom and the lavender on top (figures 24 and 25).

Figure 24

Figure 25

11. Working from the front of the work, **split the large stack** symmetrically so the three braids bend to the right and three to the left. Pick up a 4 mm bead (figure 26).

Figure 26

12. End the stack (wrap, tack, whip, and snip) around the 4 mm bead (figure 27).

Figure 27

13. Sew through the back of the work so the thread exits the other side of the join. Work as in step 12 to create a mirror on other side of the join (figures 28 and 29).

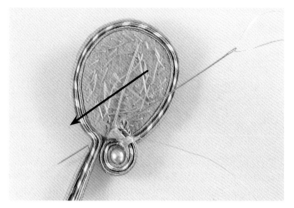

Figure 28

Figure 29

14. Using a blue 11°, an 8°, and another blue 11° seed bead, **create a bridge** at the join (figure 30).

Figure 30

15. Add a Jump ring behind the work above the join (figure 31).

Figure 31

16. Repeat steps 1 through 15 for the second earring.

Assembly and Finishing

1. Position the splash behind the bottom of the work. Secure with **tacking stitches** (figure 32).

Figure 32

2. Apply a small dab of glue on the back of the work and spread thinly, *taking care not to get any glue on the back of the splash element* (figure 33). **Apply backing.** Allow the glue to dry completely.

Figure 33

3. Trim the backing. Where the synthetic suede passes behind splash element, cut the backing in a smooth curve (figure 34).

Figure 34

4. Prepare the thread and **bury the knot** by sewing through one of the 4 mm beads near the top of the work (figure 35). Sew out through the stack at the rib.

Figure 35

5. Alternating colors of 11° seed beads, finish with **brick stitch edge beading** (figure 36). Where the edge of the backing passes behind the splash element, edge bead the edge of the backing only (figure 37). **Bury** and **trim the thread** (figure 38).

Figure 36

Figure 37

Figure 38

6. Use pliers to open the loop on an earwire. Slip the loop through the jump ring. Close the loop (figure 39).

Figure 39

7. Repeat steps 1 through 6 to make the second earring (figure 40).

Figure 40

Note: Even with such a simple design, there are many creative possibilities. Try changing the colors of the soutache and beads—see what happens (figure 41)!

Figure 41

Shimmering
Sea Turtle Pendant

Sparkling and serene, your sea turtle pendant may be the perfect talisman of tranquility.

MATERIALS & TOOLS

Beads

Aqua 14 x 15.4 mm AB briolette

2 silver 6 x 9 mm teardrop-shaped glass pearls

5 silver 7 x 12 mm teardrop-shaped glass pearls

10 turquoise 6° seed beads

1 g silver 8° seed beads

1 g silver-lined clear 8° seed beads

2 g silver-lined clear 11° seed beads

Soutache

1 yard (91.4 cm) each of BeadSmith brand ⅛-inch
 (3 mm) soutache in the following colors:

  marine

  silver gray

  linen

3 x 3-inch (7.6 x 7.6 cm) piece of powder blue
 Nicole's BeadBacking beading foundation

Gray Nymo size B beading thread

3½ inches (8.9 cm) of silver, crystal AB rhinestone
 chain (6.5 SS)

2 silver 6 mm soldered jump rings

4½ x 4½-inch (11.4 x 11.4 cm) piece of gray
 synthetic suede

18-inch (45.7 cm) silver bead chain (or link chain)

4 silver 2-inch (5.1 cm) head pins

Silver toggle clasp

Washable fiber glue

Scissors

Size 10 beading needle

Looping pliers

Flush cutters

Flat-nose or chain-nose pliers

SKILLS USED

Making a Lollipop (page 31)

Large Beads (page 55)

Working off the Beading Foundation (page 63)

Adding Soutache around Beading Foundation
 (page 65)

Steps

Prepare the Focal Bead

1. Put a small dab of glue in the center of the piece of beading foundation (figure 1). Press the briolette into the glue and set it aside to dry completely (figure 2).

Figure 1

Figure 2

2. Prepare the thread. Cut four 4-inch (10.2 cm) lengths of soutache. **Align and stack** them with marine on the bottom, then silver gray, linen, and marine. Sew up through the center of the stack (figure 3).

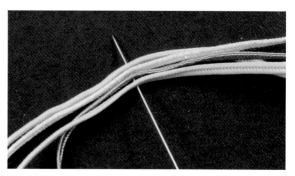

Figure 3

3. Working from right to left, make three **shaping stitches** (figure 4). Pick up a 6 x 9 mm teardrop pearl at one narrow end. Sew up through the stack close to the knot (figure 5). Follow the instructions for **Making a Lollipop** (figure 6).

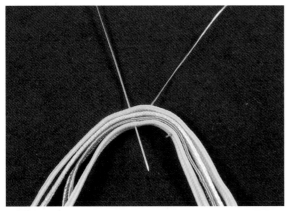

Figure 4

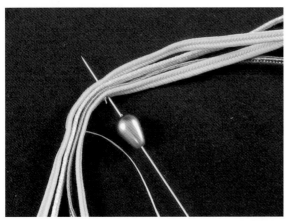

Figure 5

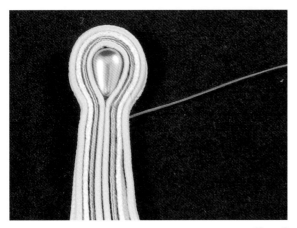

Figure 6

4. Keeping the strands straight and even, use shaping stitches to **consolidate the stack** to a length of ½ inch (1.3 cm) from the bottom of the pearl (figure 7). **Set the stitch** by sewing through the last stitch to lock it.

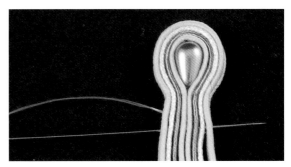

Figure 7

5. Trim the thread and the stack (figure 8).

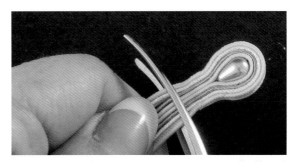

Figure 8

6. Following steps 2 through 5, use another 6 x 9 mm teardrop pearl and a 7 x 12 mm teardrop pearl to make two more lollipops (figure 9).

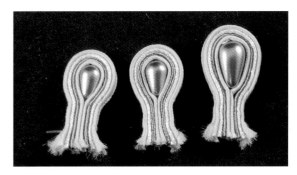

Figure 9

7. Trim the corners from the beading foundation. This makes it less likely you'll snag your thread as you're working.

8. Follow the instructions for **Large Beads** to secure the briolette to the beading foundation (figure 10).

Figure 10

9. Alternating between silver and silver-lined clear 8° seed beads, surround the briolette with a row of **backstitch 2** (figure 11). Sew through the ring of beads two or three times to smooth and tighten them (figure 12). Secure with a couple of **shallow stitches** on the back of the work (figure 13).

Figure 11

Figure 12

Figure 13

10. Drape the rhinestone chain around the ring of beads. Following the instructions for **Working off the Beading Foundation**, secure the chain to the foundation (figure 14).

Figure 14

11. Trim the beading foundation away from the work. Be careful not to overtrim—be sure leave a 1 mm border of beading foundation exposed all the way around the work (figure 15).

Figure 15

12. Prepare a new thread. Working from the back, sew into the beading foundation and through the edge so the thread is exiting the actual thickness of the beading foundation centered on the wide part of the briolette (figure 16).

Figure 16

13. Cut five 15-inch (38.1 cm) lengths of soutache, one of linen and two each of silver gray and marine. Sew through the center of one of the marine braids at the rib (figure 17). Following the instructions for **Adding Soutache around Beading Foundation**, attach the length of soutache around one side of the briolette and then the other (figure 18).

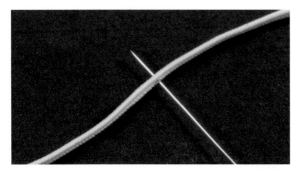

Figure 17

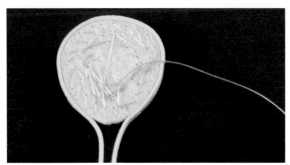

Figure 18

14. Pull the thread across the back of the work and sew into the beading foundation and the braid at the starting point. Pull the thread across the back of the work and sew into the beading foundation and the braid at the starting point (figure 19).

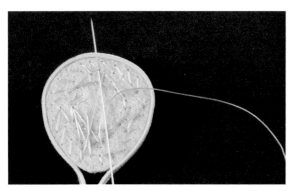

Figure 19

15. Align and stack the remaining four lengths with silver gray on the bottom, then linen, sillver gray, and marine. Sew through the center of the stack at the rib (figure 20). Following the directions for **Adding Soutache around Beading Foundation**, secure the stack around the work (figure 21). Join the stacks at the bottom of the element by making a **two-sided join** (figure 22).

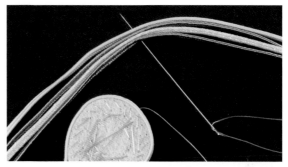

Figure 20

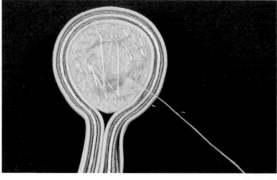

Figure 21

Figure 22

16. Working from the back, with the thread exiting left of the join, split the stack symmetrically.

17. Pick up an 8° seed bead. Create a secured **ladder** incorporating twelve 8° seed beads (figure 23).

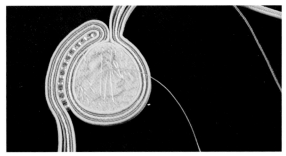

Figure 23

18. Split the working stack and continue adding four more 8° seed beads between the secured stack and the new two-layer working stack. **Set the stitch** by sewing up through the secured stack, the bead, and the working stack (figure 24).

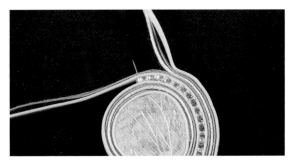

Figure 24

19. End the stack (wrap, tack, whip, and snip). Working from right to left, consolidate the stack by making four **shaping stitches** (figure 25). Wrap the working stack to the back of the work and hold it in place between your thumb and forefinger. Tack it in place with a pair of **tacking stitches** (figure 26).

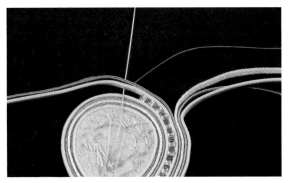

Figure 25

Figure 26

20. On the back of the work, **whipstitch** the working stack. Sew through the ribs of the working stack at the same location. Snip the ends of the soutache off of the working stack (figure 27).

Figure 27

21. To make a "flipper," sew through the back of work, the twelfth seed bead, and the outer stack (figure 28). Pick up an 8° seed bead. Fold the three-layer stack back over the last bead and sew through the stack. Set the stitch by **retracing the thread path** twice. Sew down through the working stack and bead only (figure 29).

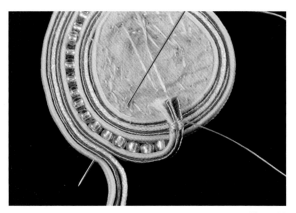

Figure 28

Figure 29

22. Pick up another 8° seed bead. Sew up through the working stack one bead width away from where the thread last entered it (figure 30). Sew down through the working stack and the last bead (figure 31).

Figure 30

Figure 31

23. Following the instructions for step 21, add another 8° seed bead, a 6° seed bead, and an 8° seed bead (figure 32).

Figure 32

24. Fold the working stack under the last 8° seed bead. Sew down through the outer stack, the 8° seed bead, and the working stack (figure 33).

Figure 33

25. Working from right to left, attach the working stack under the line of beads by sewing up through the working stack, the 6° seed bead, and the outer secured stack (figure 34), then down through the secured stack, the 8° seed bead, and the working stack (figure 35). Continue working in this fashion until the working stack is connected to all five beads in the flipper.

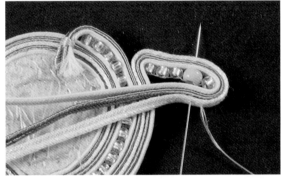

Figure 34

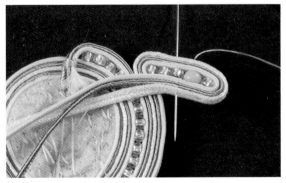

Figure 35

26. End the stack behind the work (figure 36).

Figure 36

27. Pull the thread across the back of the work. Sew into the back of the work so the thread exits the join (figure 37). Follow steps 17 through 26 to create a mirror image of the flipper on the other side (figure 38).

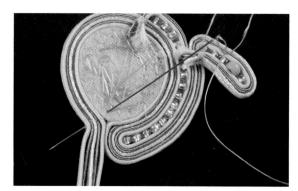

Figure 37

Figure 38

28. Place the largest lollipop behind the top of the work. Tack it in place (figure 39).

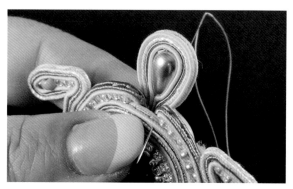

Figure 39

29. Repeat with the smaller lollipops to make rear flippers (figure 40).

Figure 40

Finishing

1. Add jump rings to the back upper edges of the work at the desired locations. **Apply backing.** Allow the glue to dry completely (figure 41).

Figure 41

2. Trim the backing.

3. Use silver-lined clear size 11° seed beads to **edge bead** with **brick stitch edge beading** (figure 42).

Figure 42

4. Cut the 18-inch (45.7 cm) chain in half.

5. Slide a 6° seed bead, a 7 x 12 mm teardrop pearl, and a 6° seed bead onto a head pin (figure 43). Use looping pliers and flush cutters to make a **bead chain link**. Repeat to make a total of four links (figure 44).

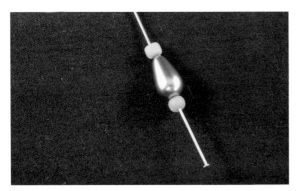

Figure 43

Figure 44

6. Use flat-nose or chain-nose pliers to open the loop on one end of a link. Attach to a jump ring and close the loop. Open the other end and attach the chain. Repeat with another link for the other jump ring and chain. Use the other two links to attach the chain ends to toggle-clasp halves (figure 45).

Figure 45

Note: This is just one sea turtle—think about what you could make with a bale of them! (Yup, a "bale" is what a group of sea turtles is called.) (figure 46).

Figure 46

Shimmering Sea Turtle Pendant **139**

Crystal Coil Earrings

This project demonstrates "endless-length" methods. These stitching techniques begin in the middle of the stack and work their way to the ends. They minimize the number of "ended" stacks and—therefore—the amount of backing and edge beading that is required. These earrings are very sparkly and lightweight, and—with endless-length methods—they work up fast!

MATERIALS & TOOLS

Beads

62 dark red 4 mm AB bicone crystals

6 wine 6 mm satin-finish glass pearls

2 wine 8 mm satin-finish glass pearls

1 g copper matte metallic 11° seed beads

0.5 g burgundy 15° seed beads

Soutache

1 yard (91.4 cm) each of BeadSmith brand ⅛-inch (3 mm) soutache in the following colors:

    merlot

    textured metallic copper

    merlot and rose stripe

    rose

Mauve Nymo size B beading thread

2 antique brass 6 mm soldered jump rings

2 x 2-inch (5.1 x 5.1 cm) piece of wine synthetic suede

Pair of antique brass earwires

Size 10 beading needle

Scissors

Washable fiber glue

Chain-nose or flat-nose pliers

SKILLS USED

Making an Independent Curved Ladder (page 41)

Making a Lollipop (page 31)

Picot (page 88)

Steps

1. Prepare the thread. Cut four 18-inch (45.7 cm) lengths of soutache, one each of merlot, textured metallic copper, merlot and rose stripe, and rose.

2. Align and stack them in that order (merlot on the bottom). Sew up through the center of the stack at the rib.

3. Retrace the thread path (figure 1).

Figure 1

4. Fold the stack over the knot. Pick up a 4 mm bicone. Sew up through the stack directly above where the thread last exited (figure 2). **Retrace the thread path** through the upper stack, bead, and lower stack (figure 3).

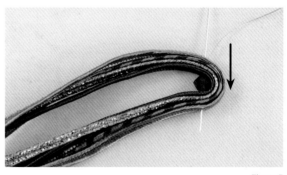

Figure 2

Figure 3

5. Following the directions for **Making Independent Curved Ladders**, make an **invisible shaping stitch** up through the lower stack. Pick up a 4 mm crystal and sew up through the upper stack approximately one-and-a-half bead widths away from where the thread entered the first bead (figure 4).

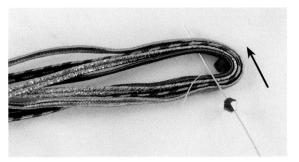

Figure 4

6. Retrace the thread path through the upper stack, bead, and lower stack (figure 5).

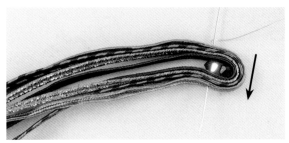

Figure 5

Note: If you're thinking of the two stacks as running parallel, you can consider the thread to be running between the lower stack and the upper stack on a 45° angle. If you're holding the work in a curve, you can consider the thread to be running "straight up and down" between the two stacks (figure 6).

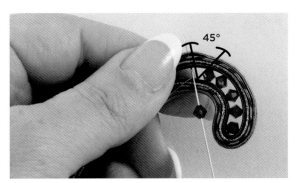

Figure 6

7. Repeat steps 5 and 6 another 28 times for a total of 30 crystals in the coil.

Note: Keep the curve tight and consistent. You will reach a point where the coil will begin to overlap itself (figure 7). Don't let that throw you—just continue to build the curve so you have an overlap of approximately half the circumference. Take the needle off but don't trim the thread.

Figure 7

8. Repeat steps 4 through 7 to make an identical coil. To make the second coil become a mirror of the first one, simply push the closed end of the ladder under the open end (figure 8). Flip the coil over and—voilà!—a mirror image (figure 9).

Figure 8

Figure 9

9. To finish each coil, pick up a 6 mm pearl and **end the stack** (figure 10). Pull the thread across back of the work and sew through the stack so the thread exits the stack just outside of last bicone. Pick up another 6 mm pearl and end the stack (figure 11).

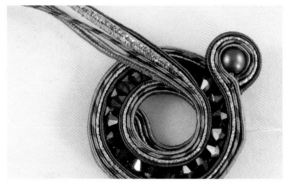

Figure 12

Figure 10

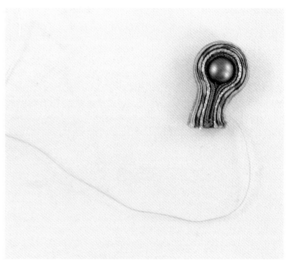

Figure 13

Figure 11

10. When you ended the stacks, one of the stacks you snipped off was much longer than the other. This is because it formed the smaller inside coil stack. Take the longer offcuts and align and stack them with the wine on the bottom, then metallic copper, the stripe, and rose. Using a 6 mm pearl, **make a lollipop** (figure 12). Trim the stack ends ¼ inch (6 mm) below the join (figure 13). **Tack** the lollipop behind the two ended stacks on the top of the coil (figure 14).

Figure 14

11. Add a jump ring at the top of the work (figure 15).

Figure 15

12. Apply backing, spreading glue only to the back of the lollipop and ended stacks (not on the ladder) (figure 16). Apply the work glue side down to wrong side of the synthetic suede. Allow to dry completely. **Trim the backing.** Where the backing crosses behind the ladder, simply follow the general shape of upper portion of component (figure 17).

Figure 16

Figure 17

13. Edge bead using **brick stitch edge beading** embellished with **picots** at every other pair of edge beads (figure 18). On the back of the work, where the backing crosses behind the ladder, attach edge beads to the edge of the backing only and do not embellish (figure 19). **Bury the thread** and trim it.

Figure 18

Figure 19

14. To make a single **fringe**, prepare a new thread and sew through the first bicone in the coil so the thread exits the stack on the outside of the coil (figure 20). Pick up an 11° seed bead, a bicone, an 11° seed bead, an 8 mm pearl, an 11° seed bead, and a 15° seed bead (figure 21). Sew back through the fringe, the outer stack, the bicone in the ladder, and the inner stack. Retrace the thead path through the ladder, fringe, 15° seed bead, fringe, and ladder. Take three or four stitches through the ladder to secure the thread. Trim the thread.

Crystal Coil Earrings **145**

Figure 20

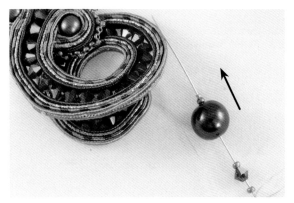

Figure 21

Note: The fringe is important in this project because it gives the bottom of the coil just enough weight to stretch, showing off the shape.

15. Use pliers to open the loop on an earwire. Attach the jump ring and close the loop (figure 22).

Figure 22

16. With second coil, repeat steps 6 through 12.

Note: These coils have many applications other than earrings. Think about incorporating them into your work so they add texture and airiness (figure 23).

Figure 23

Day of the Dead Bracelet

Celebrate Dia de los Muertos with this festival-worthy bracelet. Mix the colors randomly to get a folk art feel. Some of the flower beads are AB finish on only one side—take advantage of that by using one side in some components and the reverse side in others.

MATERIALS & TOOLS

Beads

5 cream 8 x 10 mm resin skull beads

16 red 7 mm AB Czech glass flower beads (AB on one side only)

8 purple 7 mm AB Czech glass flower beads

2 hot pink 8° seed beads

4 g salmon-lined clear 11° seed beads

5 g fuchsia transparent 15° seed beads

4 fuchsia 4 mm AB bicone crystals

4 pale green 4 mm AB bicone crystals

4 red-orange 4 mm AB bicone crystals

Soutache

1½ yards (1.4 m) each of BeadSmith brand ⅛-inch (3 mm) soutache in the following colors:

dark lilac

grass green

deep pink

red

medium blue

tyrol

lilac

goldenrod

Cathy blue size B Nymo beading thread

6 1-inch (2.5 cm) diameter soldered brass wire hoops

2 antique copper magnetic button clasps

1½ x 12-inch (3.8 x 30.5 cm) piece of fuchsia synthetic suede

Flat-nose pliers

180-grit sandpaper

Scissors

Size 10 beading needle

Washable fabric glue

SKILLS USED

Hoops (page 79)

Surface Diving (page 28)

Note: Soutache-covered hoop components can easily be added or subtracted to change the size of the bracelet. These instructions are for a six-component bracelet that will be 9½ inches (24.1 cm) long. Five components will be 8¼ inches (21 cm), and four will be 6¾ inches (17.1 cm). Need something in between? Try using four-layer stacks around the skulls, or experiment with different size hoops.

Steps

The Skull Elements

1. The backs of the skull beads are rounded, which can make it difficult to get them to sit solidly in the work. Luckily, resin sands down easily. Grip the skull face up in a pair of pliers and sand the back of the bead until it's flat (figure 1).

Figure 1

2. Prepare the thread. Cut six 6-inch (15.2 cm) lengths of soutache, two each of any three colors. **Align and stack** them so the top half of the stack mirrors the bottom half. Sew up through the stack 2 inches (5.1 cm) from the right end (figure 2). **Retrace the thread path** twice.

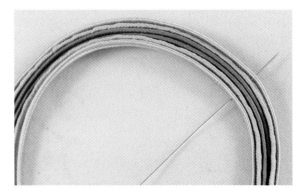

Figure 2

3. Split the left side of the stack symmetrically. Working from right to left, consolidate the upper stack with three **shaping stitches** (figure 3).

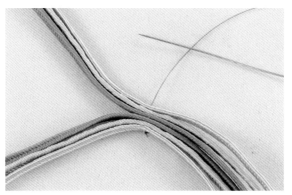

Figure 3

4. Pick up a skull bead. Sew up through the upper stack close to the join (figure 4).

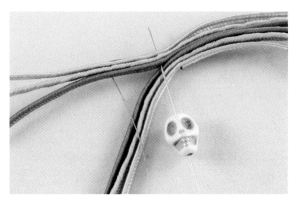

Figure 4

5. Sew down through the large stack at the **join** (figure 5).

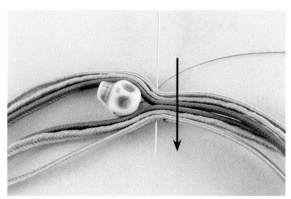

Figure 5

6. Working from right to left, consolidate the lower stack with three **shaping stitches** (figure 6).

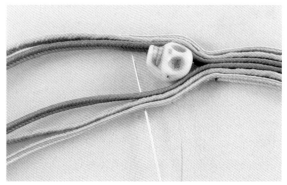

Figure 6

7. Sew through the skull bead from bottom to top (figure 7). Sew through the lower stack close to the join (figure 8). Retrace the thread path. Sew through the skull bead from top to bottom (figure 9).

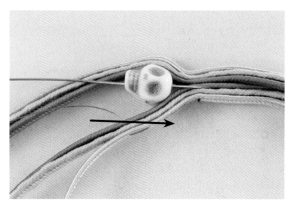

Figure 7

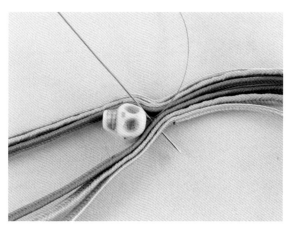

Figure 8

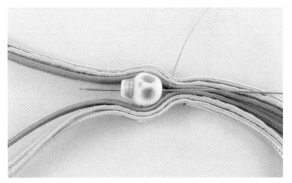

Figure 9

8. Work a **two-sided join** to the left of the skull (figure 10).

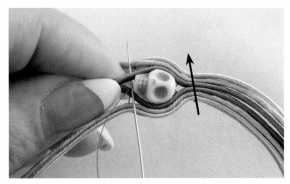

Figure 10

9. Orient the work so the skull bead is vertical. With the thread exiting right of the lower join, pick up a red flower bead (AB side down).

10. Sew through the stack where the hole of the bead naturally meets the stack (figure 11). **End the stack** (figure 12). Pull the thread across the back of the work and sew through the join so the thread exits the left side of the join. Pick up another red flower bead and make a mirror image.

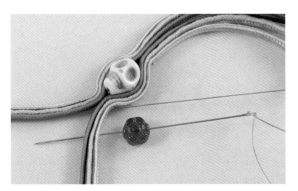

Figure 11

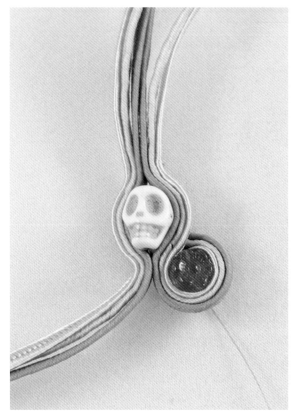

Figure 12

11. Pull thread across the back of the work and sew into the work so the thread exits right of the top join. Follow step 10 to add two more red flower beads (figure 13).

Figure 13

12. Using a 15°, 11°, and 15° seed bead, **make a bridge** below the skull. Repeat above the skull (figure 14).

Figure 14

13. Using different color combinations of soutache and different colors of flower beads, repeat steps 1 through 10 to make as many skull elements as you will need for your bracelet (figure 15).

Figure 15

The Hoop Elements

1. Cut two 8-inch (20.3 cm) lengths of any two colors of soutache. Following the directions for **Working with hoops**, wrap one of the brass hoops (figure 16).

Figure 16

2. Using different color combinations of soutache, repeat step 1 to make as many hoop elements as you will need for your bracelet.

Assembling and Finishing

1. Trim the ends of the soutache wrapping one of the hoops to a length of ¼ inch (6 mm) (figure 17).

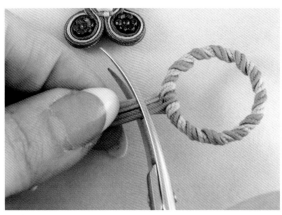

Figure 17

2. Place the cut end of the soutache wrapping the hoop behind the right side of one of the skull elements. **Tack** in place (figure 18). Repeat to combine the remaining pairs of skull components and hoops.

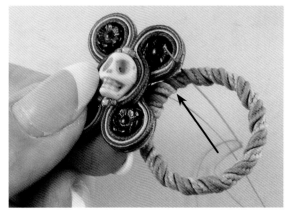

Figure 18

3. Select *one* skull-and-hoop component to be a bracelet end. **Whipstitch** a pair of magnetic clasps to the outermost corner of the stacks wrapping the flowers opposite the hoop (figure 19).

Figure 19

Note: Leave the clasp sides together just now so you don't accidentally mix up the polarities later.

4. Cut a piece of synthetic suede just larger than the skull element (figure 20).

Figure 20

5. Apply backing. When applying the glue to the back of the element, the only part of the hoop that should have glue on it is the area directly behind the skull element (figure 21). Allow the glue to dry completely.

Figure 21

6. Trim the backing (figure 22). When trimming the backing from behind the hoop, follow the line of the hoop exposing half the thickness of the wrapped hoop (figure 23).

Figure 22

Figure 23

7. Prepare a new thread and **bury the knot** by sewing through the top right flower bead and out of the stack at the rib very close to the hoop (figure 24). Using 11° seed beads, add **brick stitch edge beading** around the skull element. Where the skull element sits on top of the hoop, stitch through the hoop wrapping each time you add a bead (figure 25). Retrace the thread path through the hoop wrapping and bead, making the smallest possible stitch in the wrapping (figure 26), then add the next bead (figure 27).

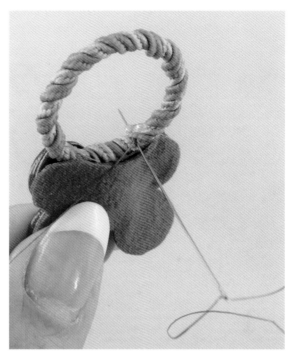

Figure 26

Figure 24

Figure 27

8. At the joins, add a decorative bicone crystal. With thread exiting the 11° seed bead in the edge beading, pick up another 11° seed bead, a bicone, and a 15° seed bead. Sew back through the bicone, the new 11° seed bead, and the 11° seed bead in the edge beading (figure 28). Continue on with the edge beading.

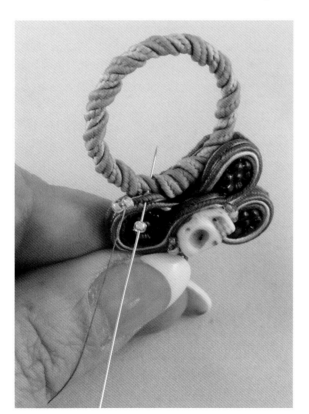

Figure 25

Figure 28

9. Where the backing runs behind a hoop, after picking up a new 11° seed bead, catch the surface of the hoop wrapping, and sew through the edge of the backing (figure 29). Complete the edge beading. **Bury the thread** (figure 30).

Figure 29

Figure 30

10. Repeat steps 1 through 8 for the remaining components (figure 31).

Figure 31

11. Prepare a new thread and bury the knot in the front of one of the components and sew through the work so the thread exits one of the edge beads below the upper right flower bead. Flip the work over (top to bottom so the ring is oriented toward the right) (figure 32). Sew through the adjacent edge bead so the thread exits between the edge bead and backing (figure 33).

Figure 32

Figure 33

12. Pick up ten 11° seed beads (figure 34). Place a second component facedown to the left and sew through the hoop. Sew into the edge bead two beads to the left of the bicone embellishment so the thread exits outside the edge beading (figure 35). Sew into the adjacent edge bead and under and out the backing (figure 36). Reinforce the seed-bead loop by retracing the thread path through the backing, out of an edge bead, into the adjacent edge bead, through the loop beads, out an edge bead, into an adjacent edge bead, and under and out the backing (figures 37 and 38).

Figure 37

Figure 34

Figure 38

13. To begin the next loop, follow the directions for **Surface Diving** underneath the backing until you are positioned to sew through the edge bead at the beginning of where the next seed-bead loop will begin (figure 39).

Figure 35

Figure 39

14. Follow step 11 to create a second diagonal seed-bead loop around the hoop (figure 40). Bury and snip the thread.

Figure 36

Figure 40

15. Follow steps steps 10 through 12 for each component (figure 41).

Figure 41

16. Separate the sides of one of the magnetic clasps. **Whipstitch** the unattached half of the clasp to the corresponding point on the hoop at the other end of the bracelet (figure 42). With thread exiting the clasp loop, pick up an 8° seed bead and a 15° seed bead. Sew down through the 8° seed bead and into the hoop wrapping outside of the clasp loop (figure 43). Retrace the thread path through the wrapping, beads, and back into the wrapping (figure 44).

Figure 42

Figure 43

Figure 44

17. Sew under the wrapping to the location for the unattached half of the second clasp and repeat step 16. Bury the thread under the wrapping and snip the thread (figure 45).

Figure 45

Note: Not feelin' it with the skull beads? No worries— the takeaway here is really all about working with the hoops. You can use the same technique with a variety of other beads (figure 46).

Figure 46

Opulent Amulet

Start with a dichroic glass cabochon and a vintage
chandelier crystal. Add a pinch of rolling waves and
a posie of lollipops. Create an alchemy of art!

MATERIALS & TOOLS

Beads

4 bronze 6 mm druk beads

20 miscellaneous beads (Select different shapes and colors in sizes ranging from 6 to 15 mm. Flat squares, disks, teardrops, and spindle beads work well. Small bead caps can also add interest. This is a great time to stir your bead soup!)

12 to 16 mm dichroic cabochon

10 red 4 mm fire-polished beads

1 g bright green 6° seed beads

1 g matte orange 8° AB seed beads

1 g matte chartreuse 8° AB seed beads

.5 g matte red translucent 11° seed beads

2 g turquoise opaque 11° seed beads

.5 g red silver-lined 15° seed beads

10 light blue 4 mm cat's-eye beads

6 yellow 4 mm cat's-eye beads

1 1 x 1½-inch (2.5 x 3.8 cm) green chandelier crystal

Soutache

2 yards (1.8 m) each of BeadSmith brand ⅛-inch (3mm) soutache in the following colors:

    red

    saffron

    celery

    dark lilac

    textured metallic copper

Mauve size B Nymo beading thread

2 x 2-inch (5.1 x 5.1 cm) piece of majestic purple Nicole's BeadBacking beading foundation

3-inch (7.6 cm) length silver, crystal AB rhinestone chain (6.5 SS)

2 gold 6 mm soldered jump rings

4½ x 4½-inch (11.4 x 11.4 cm) piece of red synthetic suede

20 gold 2-inch (5.1 cm) head pins

Gold toggle clasp

Size 10 beading needle

Scissors

Washable fiber glue

Flat-nose pliers

Looping pliers

Flush cutters

SKILLS USED

Making a Lollipop (page 31)

Peyote-Stitch Bezel (page 57)

Working off the Beading Foundation (page 63)

Adding Soutache around Beading Foundation (page 65)

Rolling Waves (page 47)

Simple Layered Connections (page 101)

Chandelier Crystal (page 76)

Rhinestone Chain (page 73)

Steps

Make Lollipops

1. **Prepare the thread.** Cut four 4-inch (10.2 cm) lengths of soutache, one each of red, saffron, celery, and dark lilac. **Align and stack** them from bottom to top in that order. Using a 6 mm druk bead, **make a lollipop** (figure 1).

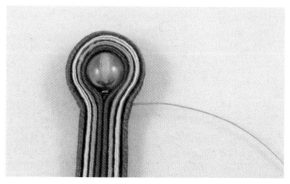

Figure 1

2. Keeping the stack straight, consolidate approximately ¾ inch (1.9 cm) of the stack by making two or three **shaping stitches** down the "stick" of the lollipop (figure 2). **Set the last stitch** by **retracing the thread path** once.

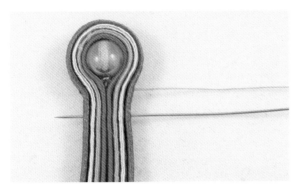

Figure 2

3. Trim the thread and the stack (figure 3).

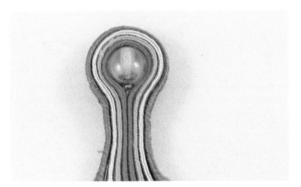

Figure 3

4. Using a variety of the miscellaneous beads, repeat steps 1 through 3 five times to make a total of six lollipops. Experiment with different shapes and stack sizes (try using five lengths of soutache instead of four). Consider adding an 8° seed bead above and below the center bead to change the shape, or add a bead cap to a round bead to create a teardrop (figure 4).

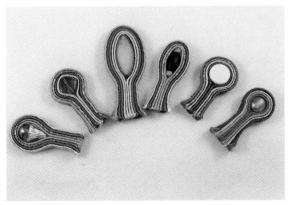

Figure 4

Prepare the Cabochon

1. Put a small drop of glue in the center of the beading foundation. Press the cabochon into the glue. Allow it to dry completely (figure 5).

Figure 5

2. Prepare the thread. Alternating colors of 11° seed beads, surround the cabochon with a row of **backstitch 2** (figure 6). This will become the base row. Secure the cabochon with a **peyote-stitch bezel**. Use red 11° seed beads to make row one. Use red 15° seed beads to make row two. Sew through all the beads in rows one and two to tighten the ring (figure 7).

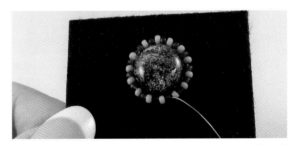

Figure 6

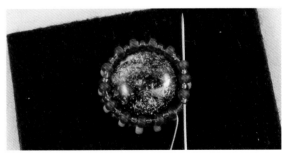

Figure 7

Opulent Amulet **163**

3. Sew down between the cabochon and bezel. Sew up through the beading foundation just outside the bezel (figure 8).

Figure 8

4. Drape the rhinestone chain around the cabochon component. Following the directions for **Working off the Beading Foundation**, attach the chain around the work (figure 9).

Figure 9

5. Trim the foundation away from the work. Be sure to leave 1 mm of foundation visible from the front of the work (figure 10).

Figure 10

Surround the Cabochon Component with Soutache

1. Cut three 20-inch (50.8 cm) lengths of soutache, one each of dark lilac, textured metallic copper, and red.

2. Prepare the thread. Sew into beading foundation behind the cabochon on a slight angle so the thread exits the very edge of the beading foundation (figure 11).

Figure 11

3. Sew through the center of the dark lilac piece of soutache at the rib (figure 12).

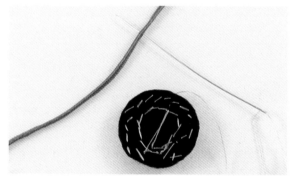

Figure 12

4. Following the directions in **Adding Soutache around Beading Foundation**, attach the dark lilac strand around the work (figure 13). Then add a stack of the remaining two strands with the textured metallic copper strand on the bottom (figure 14). Connect the stacks with a **one-sided join**.

Figure 13

Figure 14

Rolling Waves

1. Working from the back, **split the large stacks symmetrically**.

2. Pick up a 6 mm druk bead (figure 15). Sew through the stack where the bead hole meets the stack.

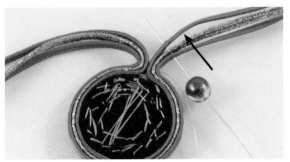

Figure 15

3. Working from left to right, make one long shaping stitch and secure the stack with a one-sided join (figure 16).

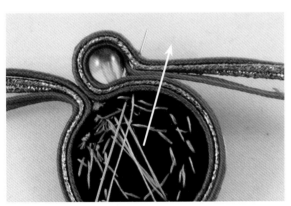

Figure 16

4. Pick up a light blue 4 mm cat's-eye bead. Following the directions for **Rolling Waves**, wrap the bead and secure the stack behind the work (figure 17).

Figure 17

5. Fold the working stack back over itself and create a **secured ladder** using seven orange 8° seed beads between the working stack and the secured stack (figure 18). Set the last stitch by retracing the thread path through the secured stack, last 8° seed bead, and the working stack twice.

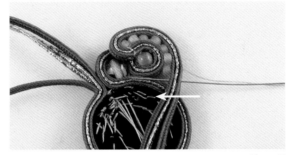

Figure 18

6. Sew down through the working stack. Pick up a bright green 6° seed bead. Sew into the secured stack surrounding the cabochon. Retrace the thread path through the secured stack, 6° seed bead, and the working stack twice (figure 19).

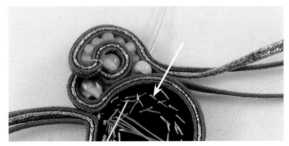

Figure 19

7. Sew through the secured stack and working stack (figure 20). Retrace the thread path twice.

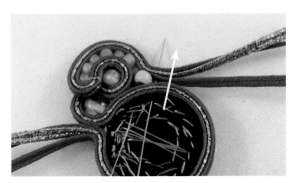

Figure 20

8. Pick up a yellow 4 mm cat's-eye bead. Follow step 4.

9. Using seven chartreuse 8° seed beads, follow steps 5 through 7 to create another rolling wave (figure 21).

Figure 21

10. Pick up a light blue 4mm cat's-eye bead and **end the stack** (figure 22).

Figure 22

11. Pull the thread across the back of the work. Sew through the work so the thread exits to the left of the join at the top of the cabochon component (figure 23).

Figure 23

12. Follow steps 2 through 10 to create a mirror image (figure 24).

Figure 24

Adding the Lollipops and Jump Rings

1. The lollipops will be attached following the directions for **Simple Layered Connections**. Place one lollipop behind the bottom center of the cabochon component (figure 25).

Figure 25

2. Use **tacking stitches** to secure it in place (figure 26).

Figure 26

3. Following steps 1 and 2, secure a lollipop on each side of the center component (figure 27).

Figure 27

4. Secure a fourth lollipop behind the center and left components. Secure a fifth behind the center and right components (figure 28).

Figure 28

5. Add the sixth lollipop at the bottom of the arrangement (figure 29).

Figure 29

6. Create a bridge at the join above the cabochon component (figure 30).

Figure 30

7. Add jump rings at the desired locations (figure 31).

Figure 31

Backing and Edge Beading

1. Apply backing but do not get glue on the lower lollipop portion of the component (figure 32). Allow the glue to dry completely.

Figure 32

2. Trim the backing (figure 33).

Figure 33

3. Prepare a new thread and **bury the knot** by sewing into the bead in the fourth lollipop and out of the stack. The knot will end up being hidden inside the bead (figure 34). With the decorative side of work facing down and working from left to right, **edge bead** using **brick stitch** (figure 35). Continue until you reach the fifth lollipop. This leaves a pocket at the bottom of the lollipop component (figure 36). Don't snip the thread.

Figure 35

Figure 36

4. Pocket the crystal following the directions for **Chandelier Crystals** (figure 37).

Figure 34

Figure 37

Chain and Assembly

1. Put a bead or selection of beads on a head pin. Following the directions for a **bead chain**, make a link (figure 38).

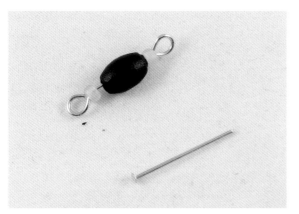

Figure 38

2. Repeat step 1 to create an identical link. Working in pairs, continue to make bead-chain links until you have enough to make two chains of the desired length.

3. Use flat-nose pliers to open and close loops and connect the link to complete the chains (figure 39). Add half of the toggle clasp to each chain (figure 40).

Figure 39

Figure 40

4. Attach one chain to each jump ring on the amulet (figure 41).

Figure 41

Note: Chandelier crystals come in many shapes and sizes. Use your imagination and think of all the ways you could incorporate them into your work (figure 42).

Figure 42

In Living Color Cuff

Packed with attitude and a variety of
techniques, including twining vine,
spike beads, and the lasagna stitch, this
funky cuff is practically a wearable sampler.

MATERIALS & TOOLS

Beads

16 metallic purple SuperDuo beads

6 blue 6 mm cat's-eye beads

3 metallic purple/gold 6 mm fire-polished beads

18 yellow 4 mm cat's-eye beads

6 red 4 mm fire-polished beads

10 silver-lined red 6° seed beads

5 matte orange 8° AB seed beads

1 g matte red translucent 11° seed beads

8 g turquoise opaque 11° seed beads

1 g silver-lined red 15° seed beads

13 x 18.5 mm blueberry Lunasoft cabochon

7 copper 7 x 17 mm spike beads

Soutache

3 yards (2.7 m) each of BeadSmith brand ⅛-inch (3 mm) soutache in the following colors:

    red

    saffron

    textured metallic copper

    celery

    dark lilac

Light purple size B Nymo beading thread

Antique copper magnetic clasp

4½ x 8½-inch (11.4 x 21.6 cm) piece of red synthetic suede

3 x 3-inch (7.6 x 7.6 cm) piece of true red Nicole's BeadBacking beading foundation

Size 10 beading needle

Scissors

Washable fabric glue

10-ounce soup can

SKILLS USED

SuperDuos (page 68)

Peyote-Stitch Bezel (page 57)

Adding Soutache around Beading Foundation (page 65)

Making a Lollipop (page 31)

Tall Beads (page 56)

Lasagna Stitch (page 35)

Zipper Edge (page 93)

Steps

Twining Vine

1. Prepare the thread. Cut five 22-inch (55.9 cm) lengths of soutache, one each of red, saffron, textured metallic copper, celery, and dark lilac. **Align and stack** them in that order (red on the bottom). Sew through the center of the stack from bottom to top.

2. Fold the stack back over the knot (figure 1).

Figure 1

3. Sew up through all the strands, keeping the needle very close to the fold (figure 2).

Figure 2

4. Retrace the thread path three times, gradually increasing thread tension to shape and tighten the fold (figure 3).

Figure 3

5. Separate the large stack into two equal stacks. Sew through the lower stack very close to the fold (figure 4).

Figure 4

6. Pick up a SuperDuo bead. (Test *both holes* of each SuperDuo to be sure they are completely open before incorporating the bead into your work.) Sew through the upper stack close to the fold (figure 5).

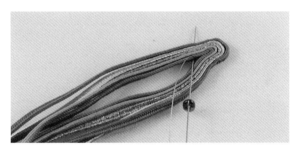

Figure 5

7. Following the directions for **SuperDuos Increase**. Sew down through the upper stack so the needle exits in line with second hole of the SuperDuo. Pick up a second SuperDuo (figure 6).

Figure 6

8. Sew through the second hole of first bead and pick up a third SuperDuo (figure 7). Sew down through the bottom stack.

Figure 7

9. Following the directions for **SuperDuos Decrease**. Sew up through the bottom stack so the needle exits in line with the second hole of the third bead. Sew through the second hole of the third bead (figure 8). Pick up a fourth SuperDuo and sew through the second hole of the second bead and the upper stack.

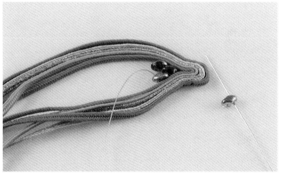

Figure 8

10. Sew down through the upper stack so the needle exits in line with the second hole of the fourth bead. Sew through the second hole of the fourth bead and the lower stack (figure 9).

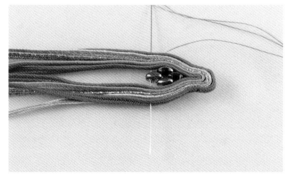

Figure 9

11. Sew up through the lower and upper stacks just beyond the last bead. **Set the stitch** by retracing the thread path twice (figure 10).

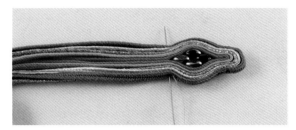

Figure 10

12. Flip the work over so the thread is exiting the bottom of the work. **Train** the large stack to the left (figure 11).

Figure 11

13. Pick up a blue 6 mm bead and sew through the large stack where the bead hole meets the stack (figure 12).

Figure 12

14. Set the stitch by retracing the thread path twice (figure 13).

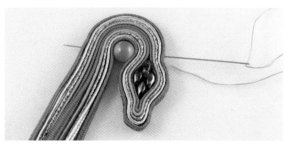

Figure 13

15. Sew back through the left stack so the thread exits one half a 6° seed bead away from surface of the 6 mm bead. Pick up a red 6° seed bead (figure 14) and sew through the stack left of the SuperDuo configuration (figure 15). Set the stitch by retracing the thread path once through the secured stack, 6° seed bead, and working stack (figure 16).

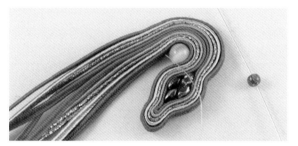

Figure 14

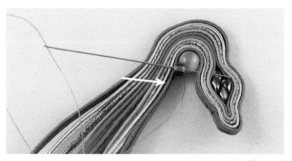

Figure 15

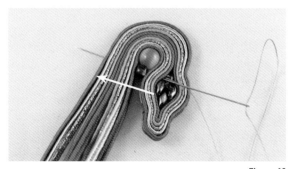

Figure 16

16. Sew through the large stack just beyond the 6° seed bead (figure 17). Set the stitch by retracing the thread path twice so that thread is exiting bottom of working stack (in between working stack and SuperDuo element), just beyond 6° seed bead.

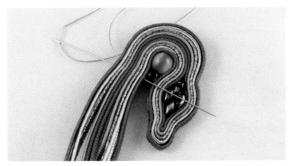

Figure 17

17. Repeat steps 5 through 16 three times (if your wrist is *very* small, only repeat twice). Retrace the thread path so the thread exits above the large stack (figure 18).

Figure 18

18. Separate the large stack into two equal stacks. Pick up a 4 mm faceted bead and **end the stack** (wrap, tack, whip, and snip) (figure 19).

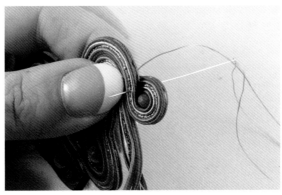

Figure 19

19. Pull the thread across the back of the work and sew through the stack so the thread exits very close to the join (figure 20).

Figure 20

20. Using a turquoise 11° seed bead, an 8° seed bead, 6° seed bead, 8° seed bead, and turquoise 11° seed bead, make a **ladder** that increases then decreases in width between the **secured stack** and the working stack (figure 21).

Figure 21

21. Make four **shaping stitches** and end the stack (figure 22).

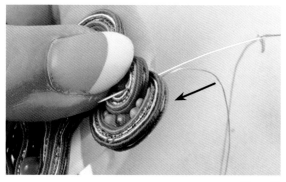

Figure 22

22. Sew one half of the magnetic clasp where the working stack of the ladder wraps behind the work (figure 23). **End the thread.**

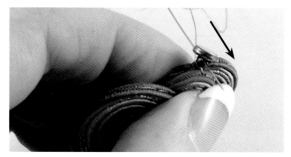

Figure 23

23. Apply backing. Apply glue to the back of the work (figure 24) and adhere it to the wrong side of the synthetic suede (figure 25). Allow the glue to dry completely.

Figure 24

Figure 25

Cabochon Component

1. Glue the cabochon to the beading foundation. Allow the glue to dry completely (figure 26).

Figure 26

2. Secure the cabochon with a **peyote-stitch bezel**. Prepare the thread and sew up through the beading foundation very close to the cabochon.

3. Alternating between turquoise and red 11° seed beads, surround the cabochon with **backstitch 2** (figures 27 and 28) to make the base row. Sew through the entire base row to smooth and tighten the ring.

Figure 27

Figure 28

4. Follow the directions for **Peyote Stitch Bezel**, step up and use turquoise 11° seed beads to make row one. Step up again and use red 15° seed beads to make row two (figure 29).

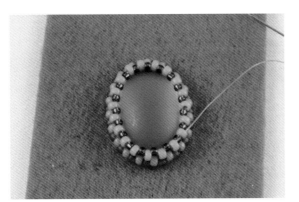

Figure 29

5. Sew through all the beads in row one and two to tighten the bezel (figure 30).

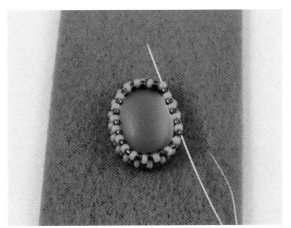

Figure 30

6. Sew down through the bezel and beading foundation (figure 31). Secure the thread by making a couple of **shallow stitches** in the back of the work.

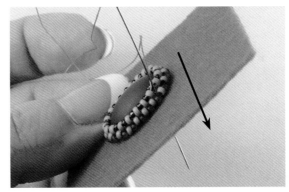

Figure 31

7. Sew up through the beading foundation close to the work. Using **backstitch 2**, surround the cabochon with a row of yellow 4 mm cat's-eye beads (figure 32). Sew through all the 4 mm beads to smooth and tighten the circle. Sew down through the beading foundation. Secure the thread by taking a couple of shallow stitches in the back of work.

Figure 32

8. Trim the foundation (figure 33).

Figure 33

9. Cut four 8½-inch (21.6 cm) lengths of soutache, two each of red and dark lilac.

10. Working from the back, orient the work so one of the wide sides is up. Sew through the beading foundation so the needle exits the *very edge* of beading foundation at the top center of the work (figure 34). Following the directions for **Adding Soutache around Beading Foundation**, attach one of the red strands first (figure 35), then the stack of one red (on the bottom) and two dark lilac strands (figure 36). Make a **two-sided join** at the bottom of the work.

Figure 34

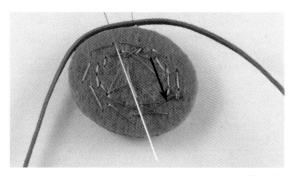

Figure 35

Figure 36

11. Rotate the work so the working stacks are at the top of the work and the thread is exiting the right side of the join. Divide the large stack into two equal stacks. Pick up a yellow 4 mm bead and end the stack (figure 37). Pull the thread across the back of the work and sew through the join so the thread exits the join on the left. Pick up a 4 mm bead and end the stack to make a mirror image (figure 38).

Figure 37

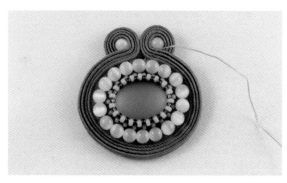

Figure 38

12. Use a turquoise 11° seed bead, an 8° seed bead, and a turquoise 11° seed bead to **create a bridge** at the join (figure 39).

Figure 39

13. Embellish with **couching**. Sew through the back of the work so the thread exits between the bezel and the 4 mm beads directly behind where two of the 4 mm beads touch (figure 40).

Figure 40

14. Pick up seven 15° seed beads. Sew over the 4 mm beads and into the beading foundation (figure 41). Repeat all the way around the circle of 4 mm beads (figure 42).

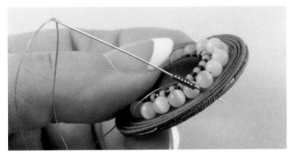

Figure 41

Figure 42

15. Working from the back, sew through the stack surrounding the right 4 mm bead so the thread exits the rib of the outermost strand very close to the join (figure 43).

Figure 43

16. Pick up an 8° seed bead. Cut three 6-inch (15.2 cm) lengths of soutache, one each of celery, textured metallic copper, and saffron. Align and stack them in that order (celery on the bottom). Sew through the center of the stack (figure 44).

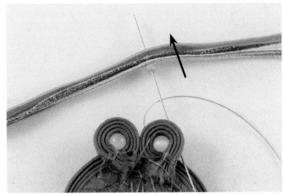

Figure 44

17. Sew back through the stack and the 8° seed bead and into the stack wrapping the left 4 mm bead (figure 45).

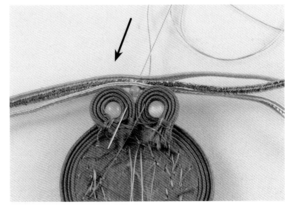

Figure 45

18. Use **shaping stitches** to secure the working stack around the secured stack wrapping the left 4 mm bead (figure 46). At the plane change, sculpt the working stack to follow the upper plane (figure 47). Set the stitch by retracing the thread path (figure 48).

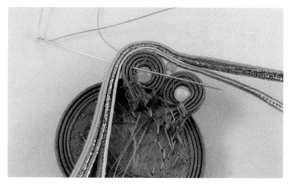

Figure 46

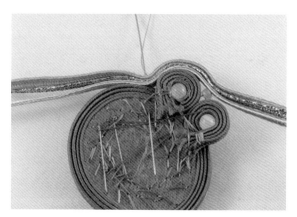

Figure 47

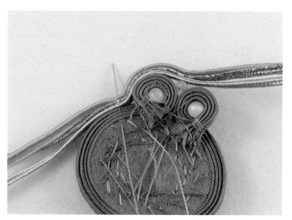

Figure 48

19. Pick up a red 4 mm faceted bead and end the stack (figure 49).

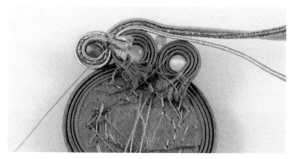

Figure 49

20. Working from back, sew through the **whipstitches** of the last ended stack (figure 50).

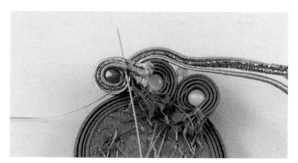

Figure 50

21. Cut three 4-inch (10.2 cm) lengths of celery soutache. **Align and stack** them. Sew through the stack 1 inch (2.5 cm) from the right end (figure 51).

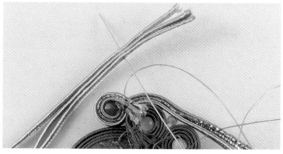

Figure 51

22. Use **shaping stitches** to attach the stack around the secured stack, wrapping the 4 mm faceted bead (figure 52). Secure the working stack to the stack wrapping the center cabochon (figure 53). Set the stitch by retracing the thread path.

Figure 52

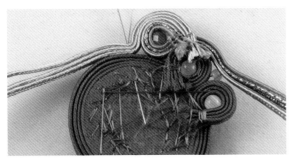

Figure 53

23. Pick up a 4 mm faceted bead and end the stack (figure 54).

Figure 54

24. Cut three 4-inch (10.2 cm) lengths of soutache, one each of dark lilac, textured metallic copper, and saffron. Align and stack them in that order (purple on the bottom). Follow steps 21 through 23 (figure 55).

Figure 55

25. Pull the thread across the back of the work to the top. Repeat steps 18 through 24 to create a mirror image on the other side of the work (figure 56).

Figure 56

26. Prepare a new thread.

27. Cut five 8-inch (20.3 cm) lengths of soutache, one each of all five colors. Align and stack them with dark lilac on the bottom, then celery, textured metallic copper, saffron, and red. Sew up through the center of the stack from the bottom, keeping the ribs aligned

28. Make a lollipop around a 6 mm faceted bead (figure 57).

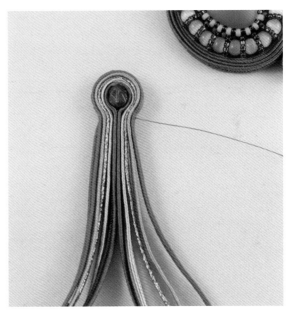

Figure 57

29. With the thread exiting left of the join, train the large stack to the left (figure 58).

Figure 58

30. Pick up a spike bead and sew through the stack where the bead hole meets the stack (figure 59). Set the stitch by retracing the thread path twice.

Figure 59

31. Working from right to left, make four **shaping stitches** and end the stack behind the work (figure 60).

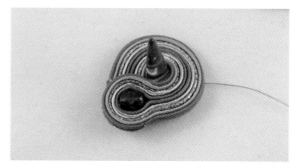

Figure 60

32. Following the directions for **Tall Beads**, secure the spike bead with a **peyote-stitch bezel** (figure 61) comprised of a base row and row one of of turquoise 11° seed beads and row two of red 15° seed beads.

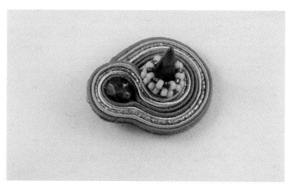

Figure 61

33. Repeat steps 26 through 32, but add the spike bead upside down and end the stack *in front* of the work in step 30 to create a mirror image (figure 62).

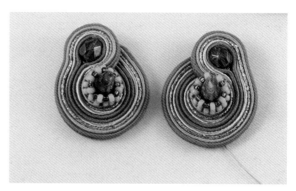

Figure 62

34. Use **tacking stitches** to secure each spike element behind the cabochon element as shown (figure 63).

Figure 63

Lasagna Stitch Component

1. Prepare a new thread.

2. Cut nine 11-inch (27.9 cm) lengths of soutache, two each of all four solid colors and one of metallic.

3. Align and stack them with saffron on the bottom then saffron, red, textured metallic copper, red, celery, celery, dark lilac, and dark lilac. Sew through the center of the stack from bottom to top, keeping the ribs aligned. Make a lollipop around a 6 mm faceted bead (figure 64).

Figure 64

4. Rotate the work so the bead is pointed to the right and the thread is exiting at the bottom of the join. Separate the large stack so six strands are on the bottom and 12 are on top. Sew up through the bottom stack, keeping the needle close to the join (figure 65).

Figure 65

5. Pick up an 8° seed bead. Separate the upper stack into two equal stacks. Sew through the first six-layer stack (figure 66).

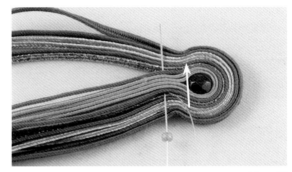

Figure 66

6. Pick up an 8° seed bead. Sew through the upper stack (figure 67).

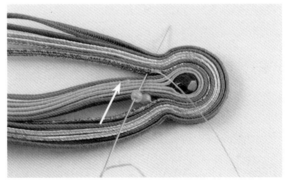

Figure 67

7. Retrace the thread path through all the stacks and beads (figure 68).

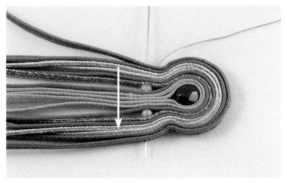

Figure 68

8. Separate the bottom stack into two equal stacks (figure 69). Sew through the bottom stack, keeping the needle close to the join. Pick up an 8° seed bead.

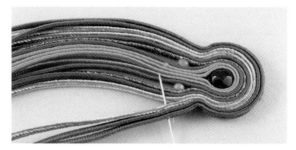

Figure 69

9. Sew through the upper stack. Separate the next stack up into two equal stacks. Sew through the lower stack (figure 70).

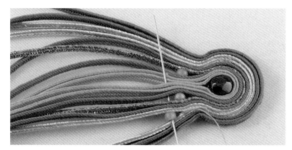

Figure 70

10. Pick up an 8° seed bead. Repeat step 9 (figure 71).

Figure 71

11. Pick up an 8° seed bed. Sew through the upper stack. Retrace the thread path (figure 72).

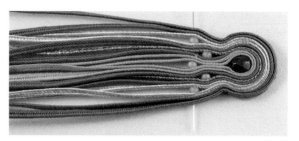

Figure 72

12. Following the directions for **Lasagna Stitch**, split and redistribute stacks to add a row of two 6° seed beads, a row of three 6° seed beads, a row of two spikes, and a row of three spikes (figure 73).

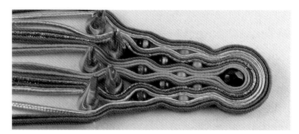

Figure 73

13. One by one, secure the spikes by splitting and redistributing stacks and making two-sided joins (figure 74). You will have to trace a path between areas to position your needle to begin each join (figures 75 and 76).

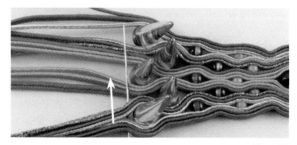

Figure 74

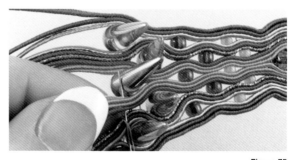

Figure 75

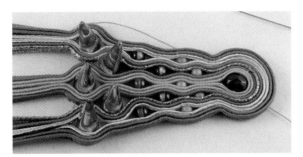

Figure 76

14. Following step 32 of **Cabochon Component**, secure each spike with a peyote-stitch bezel (figure 77).

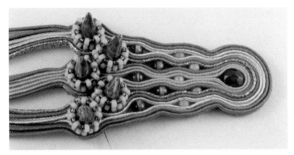

Figure 77

15. Sew through all three stacks (figure 78). Set the stitch by retracing the thread path. Make a couple of shaping stitches along the length of the large stack for about ¾ inch (1.9 cm). Trim the stack (figure 79).

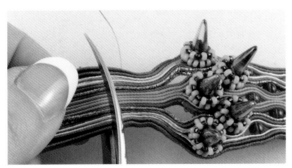

Figure 78

Figure 79

Assemble and Finish the Components

1. Position the lasagna stitch component behind the cabochon component. Secure with **tacking stitches** (figure 80). Sew the other half of the magnetic clasp to the faceted bead end of the lasagna component.

Figure 80

2. Cut a piece of synthetic suede roughly the shape of the component (figure 81).

Figure 81

3. Apply backing. While the glue is still wet, lay the component over a 10-ounce soup can (figure 82). Allow the glue to dry completely.

Figure 82

4. Trim the backing from each component (figure 83).

Figure 83

5. Using turquoise 11° seed beads, finish each component with **zipper-edge-style edge beading** (figure 84).

Figure 84

6. Connect the magnets (figure 85).

Figure 85

7. Fit the bracelet around your wrist. The end of bracelet can overlap the cabochon component as much or as little as is needed to for a correct fit (figure 86).

Figure 86

8. Remove the bracelet and replace the overlap as it was positioned on your wrist (figure 87).

Figure 87

Figure 89

Note: Spikes a little more attitude than you're comfortable with? Just swap 'em out for some 6 mm round beads.

9. Sew through the back of the bracelet end (figure 88). Secure it to the top of the cabochon component with tacking stitches (figure 89). (Keep stitches on back of synthetic suede very small.)

Figure 88

Classic Convertible Earrings

Whether you're going business casual or black tie,
you'll arrive in style—these earrings come
fully loaded with fabulous features, including
"power buttons" to get you the very best mileage!

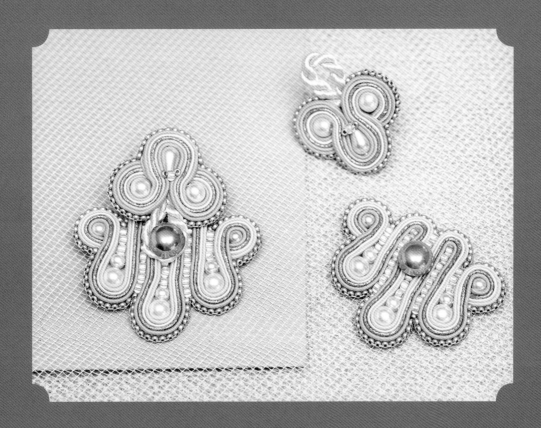

Materials & Tools

Beads

2 bronze 7 x 12 mm teardrop-shaped glass pearls

10 gold 6 mm glass pearls

6 gold 6° matte seed beads

3 g metallic burgundy 8° seed beads

2 g matte gold 11° seed beads

8 silver-lined wine 15° seed beads

2 13 mm mother-of-pearl buttons with shanks

6 bronze metallic 6 x 4mm fire-polished rondelles

4 matte gold 4 mm fire-polished beads

6 honey 5 x 7 mm teardrop-shaped crystals

Soutache

BeadSmith brand ⅛-inch (3 mm) soutache (tightly braided, 2.5 mm wide) in the following amounts and colors:

   3 yards (2.7 m) of merlot

   2 yards (1.8 m) of light brown

   2 yards (1.8 m) of textured metallic bronze

   2 yards (1.8 m) of beaver brown

   2 yards (1.8 m) of beige

Brown size B Nymo beading thread

6 inches of pale gold twisted cord

Pair of earring posts with 10 mm flat pads and earring backs

4½ x 4½ -inch (11.4 x 11.4 cm) piece of tan synthetic suede

Size 10 beading needle

Scissors

Washable fabric glue

Darning needle

SKILLS USED

Make a Lollipop (page 31)

Ladders (page 40)

Fringe (page 90)

Surface Diving (page 28)

Steps

Post Components

1. Prepare the thread. Cut six 6-inch (15.2 cm) lengths of soutache, two of merlot, one of light brown, one of textured metallic bronze, one of beaver brown, and one of beige. **Align and stack** them with the merlot on the bottom, then light brown, textured metallic bronze, beaver brown, beige, and merlot. Sew through the center of the stack from bottom to top (figure 1).

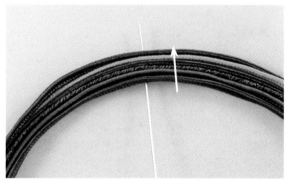

Figure 1

2. Using a 7 x 12 mm bronze teardrop pearl and sewing into narrow end first, **make a lollipop** (figure 2).

Figure 2

3. Turn the work so the bead is oriented toward you. Separate the stack symmetrically. Pick up a 6 mm gold pearl (figure 3).

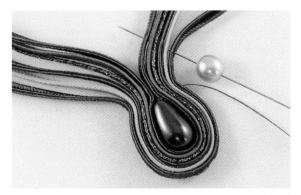

Figure 3

4. End the stack. Pull the thread across the back of work. Sew through the work so the thread exits left of the join. Pick up a 6 mm pearl and end the stack to mirror the right side (figure 4).

Figure 4

5. With an 11° seed bead, an 8° seed bead, and an 11° seed bead, **create a bridge** at the join (figure 5). Trim the thread.

Figure 5

6. Prepare a new thread. Cut a 3-inch (7.6 cm) length of twisted cord. Fold the cord in half. Sew through both ends of the cord near the cut ends (figure 6). Working from left to right, sew the cord ends together using small **shaping stitches** (figure 7). As the loop starts to get smaller, test the fit loop by passing a button through it (figure 8). Continue making small running stitches until the loop is *just* large enough to pass the button through. **Set the stitch** by sewing through both cord ends twice.

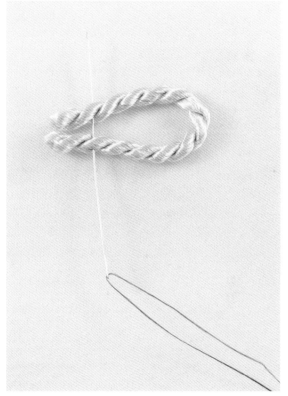

Figure 6

Figure 7

Figure 8

7. Place the loop behind the join of the soutache component and **tack** it in place (figure 9).

Figure 9

8. Place a drop of glue on the back of the soutache component near the wide end of the teardrop-shaped pearl bead. Gently press the pad of the earring post into the glue (figure 10). Allow it to dry completely.

Figure 10

9. Cut a piece of synthetic suede just larger than the soutache component. Press a darning needle through the suede at the location the post would pass through (figure 11). Slip the post through hole to make sure the component fits on the backing. (If your component is off the backing, adjust by making a new hole; the synthetic suede will "heal.")

Figure 11

10. Apply backing. Do not get glue on the twisted cord (figure 12).

Figure 12

11. Press the post through the synthetic suede (figure 13). Allow the glue to dry completely.

Figure 13

12. Trim the backing. Where the backing passes behind the loop, follow the shape of the soutache, allowing the loop to hang free of backing.

13. Edge bead using **brick stitch** edge beading (figure 14). Where the edge of the backing passes behind the loop, edge bead only the edge of the backing (figure 15).

Figure 14

Figure 15

14. Repeat steps 1 through 13 to make a second component.

Button-On Extensions

1. Prepare a new thread. Cut five 15-inch (38.1 cm) lengths of soutache, one each of beige, beaver brown, textured metallic bronze, light brown, and merlot. Align and stack them in that order, with beige on the bottom. Sew up through the center of the stack at the rib.

2. Working from left to right, take one **shaping stitch** (figure 16).

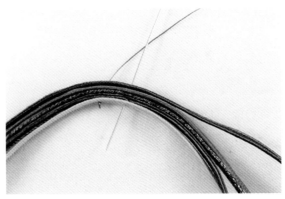

Figure 16

3. Pick up a 6 mm gold pearl and sew through the stack directly across from where the thread last exited (figure 17).

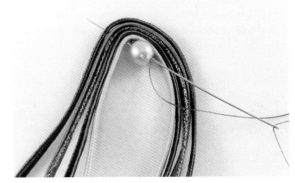

Figure 17

4. Orient the work so the bead is pointed right and **retrace the thread path** back down through the top stack, bead, and the bottom stack (figure 18).

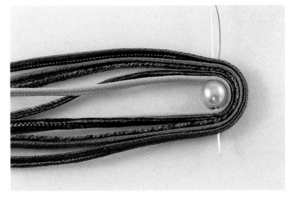

Figure 18

5. Using a rondelle, a 6° seed bead, and four 8° seed beads, make a **straight independent graduated ladder** (figure 19).

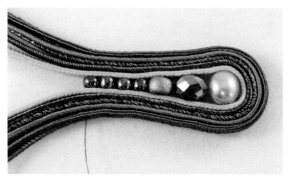

Figure 19

6. Sew up through the lower stack. Pick up a button (figure 20). Sew up through the upper stack (figure 21). Retrace the thread path through the upper stack, button, and lower stack (figure 22).

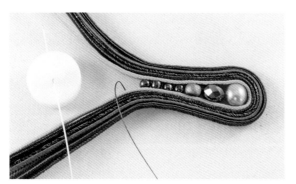

Figure 20

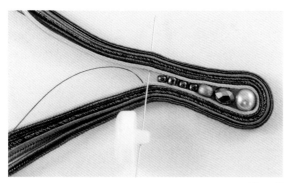

Figure 21

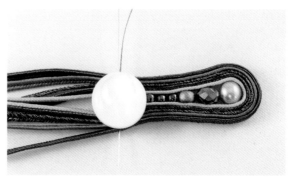

Figure 22

7. Working from right to left, continue the stack with three more 8° seed beads (figure 23). (*This photo shows work as viewed from the back.*)

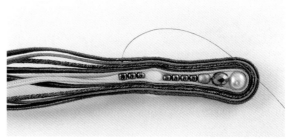

Figure 23

8. With thread exiting bottom of work, pickup an 8° seed bead. Fold the stack around the bead and sew through the stack (figure 24). Working from left to right, use 10 more 8° seed beads to create a **straight secured parallel ladder** between the working stack and the secured stack (figure 25).

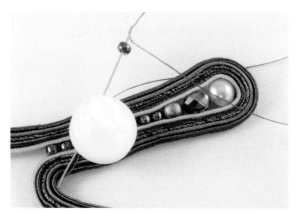

Figure 24

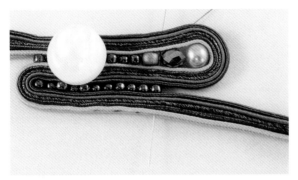

Figure 25

9. With the thread exiting the bottom of the work, pick up a 6 mm pearl. Fold the stack around pearl and sew through the stack (figure 26). Using a rondelle, a 6° seed bead, and three 8° seed beads, make a **straight secured graduated ladder** (figure 27).

Figure 26

Figure 27

10. Pick up a 4 mm fire-polished bead (figure 28) and **end the stack** (figure 29).

Figure 28

Figure 29

11. Pull thread across the back of the work and sew through the upper stack near the end of the first ladder. Work as in steps 8 through 10 to create a mirror image (figure 30). **End the thread.**

Figure 30

12. Apply backing. Edge bead using **brick stitch edge beading** (figure 31).

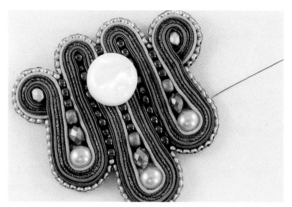

Figure 31

13. On the back of the work, **bury the thread** by sewing underneath some of the blanket stitches formed by the edge-beading process until you reach the center bottom of the left-hand lobe (figure 32).

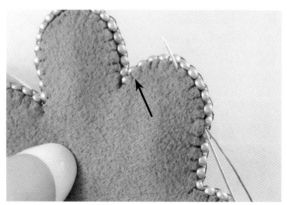

Figure 32

14. Sew out through the center edge bead (figure 33). Following the directions for **fringe**, pick up an 11° seed bead, an 8° seed bead, an 11° seed bead, a teardrop crystal (sew into narrow end first), and a 15° seed bead. Sew back through all beads except the 15° seed bead, into the edge bead, and through the backing (figure 34).

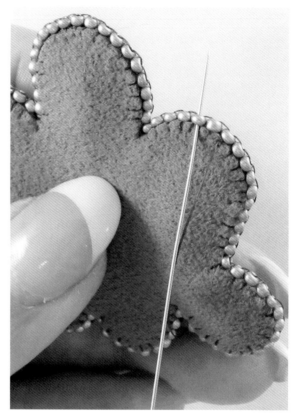

Figure 33

Figure 34

15. To get to the location for the next fringe, you can either continue burying the thread under the blanket stitches or you can **surface dive** across by taking a tiny stitch down into the backing and sliding the needle under the backing (figure 35).

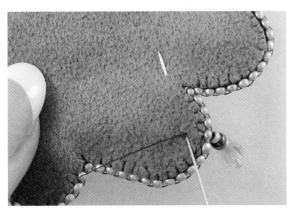

Figure 35

16. Following step 14, add a fringe to the bottom of the two other lower lobes (figure 36). Bury and snip the thread.

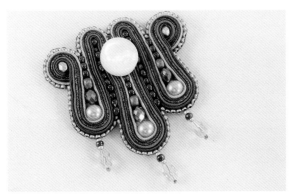

Figure 36

17. Repeat steps 1 through 16 to make a second component.

18. Post portions can be worn alone (figure 37) or with the extensions buttoned on (figure 38).

Figure 37

Figure 38

Note: If these earrings are larger than you'd like, this is a great opportunity to get a better understanding of just how much stack sizes can affect the overall size and look of your work. While these earrings were made with six-layer stacks for the top portions and five-layer stacks for the bottom, the smaller, cream-colored earrings were achieved by working exactly the same way but with five- and four-layer stacks (figure 39). What would happen if you changed the stack sizes further? Or changed the bead sizes or shapes?

Figure 39

The Impossible Romance Necklace

While I love making soutache jewelry that's all about the soutache, sometimes other elements need to be allowed to shine. These hand-carved, hand-painted porcelain cabochons by artist Stephanie Young of Calmwater Designs are a perfect example.
The night-loving moth and sun-worshiping butterfly would most likely never meet, but they looked so lovely together, I couldn't bear to separate them.
The story of their impossible romance needs little more than a frame, and soutache lends itself graciously to this application.

MATERIALS & TOOLS

Beads

2 12 mm round cabochons

1 30 x 55 mm cabochon

1 55 mm round cabochon

12 matte olive green 6° seed beads

12 matte olive green 8° seed beads

4 g beige-lined translucent seafoam 11° seed beads

2 g pearl sage 11° seed beads

0.5 g silver-lined blue 15° seed beads

8 silver 4 mm glass pearls

6 silver 6 mm glass pearls

7 x 12 silver mm glass teardrop-shaped pearl

2 silver 6 x 9 mm glass teardrop-shaped pearls

2 silver 5 x 7 mm glass teardrop-shaped pearls

Soutache

BeadSmith brand ⅛-inch (3 mm) soutache in the following amounts and colors:

    2 yards (1.8 m) sage

    2 yards (1.8 m) ivy and celery stripe

    4 yards (3.7 m) celery

4½ x 9-inch (11.4 x 22.9 cm) piece of powder blue Nicole's BeadBacking beading foundation

Olive size B Nymo beading thread

2 antique silver 6 mm soldered jump rings

4½ x 9-inch (11.4 x 22.9 cm) piece of green synthetic suede

4 silver 2-inch (5.1 cm) 21-gauge head pins

2 antique silver 10-inch (25.4 cm) four-strand chains

Antique silver toggle clasp

Washable fiber glue

Size 10 beading needle

Scissors

Flat-nose or chain-nose pliers

Looping pliers

Flush cutters

SKILLS USED

Peyote-Stitch Bezel (page 57)

Adding Soutache around Beading Foundation (page 65)

Making a Lollipop (page 31)

Simple Layered Connections (page 101)

Beaded/Sewn Connections (page 96)

Surface Diving (page 28)

Bead Chain (page 12)

Note: Stephanie Young of Calmwater Designs (www.calmwaterdesigns.com) is an internationally renowned porcelain artist best known for her contemporary take on art nouveau style.

Steps

1. Following the directions for **Cabochons**, glue all the cabochons to the beading foundation. Use seafoam 11° seed beads and 15° seed beads to secure each cabochon to the beading foundation with a **peyote-stitch bezel** (figure 1). **Trim the foundation.**

Figure 1

2. Prepare the thread. Cut four 8-inch (20.3 cm) lengths of soutache, one of sage, one of ivy and celery stripe, and two of celery. Following the directions for **Adding Soutache around Beading Foundation**, sew through the beading foundation of one of the 12 mm cabochons so that the thread exits the edge of the foundation. Locate the center of the sage strand of soutache. Following the directions for **making a lollipop**, attach it around the beading foundation (figure 2).

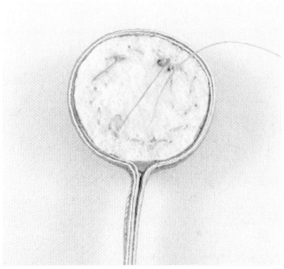

Figure 2

3. Align and stack the remaining three pieces of soutache with the celery on the bottom, then the stripe, and finally the celery. Locate the center of the stack. Following the directions for **Adding Soutache around Beading Foundation**, attach the stack around the work (figure 3).

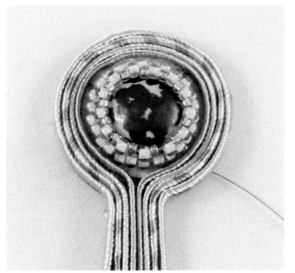

Figure 3

4. Rotate the work so the cabochon is oriented toward you. Split the stack symmetrically. Pick up a 4 mm bead. Sew through the stack where the bead hole naturally meets the stack. **End the stack** (figure 4).

Figure 4

5. Sew through the work so that the thread exits work just left of the join. Pick up another 4 mm bead and end the stack (figure 5).

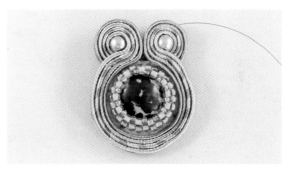

Figure 5

6. Use a 15° seed bead, a seafoam 11° seed bead, and another 15° seed bead to **create a bridge** over the join (figure 6).

Figure 6

7. Repeat steps 1 through 6 to frame the second 12 mm cabochon.

8. Follow steps 1 through 6 to frame the 30 x 55 mm cabochon but in step 2, cut the four lengths of soutache to 12 inches (30.5 cm) and begin attaching the soutache at the center *bottom* of the cabochon (figure 7). When creating the bridge, use two seafoam 11° seed beads, two 8° seed beads, and a 6° seed bead.

Figure 7

9. Following steps 1 through 3, frame the 55 mm cabochon but in step 2, cut the four lengths of soutache to 18 inches (45.7 cm) and begin attaching the soutache at the center bottom of the cabochon (figure 8).

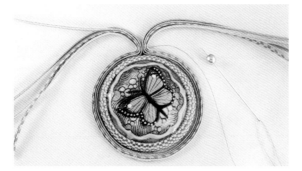

Figure 8

10. Rotate the work so the cabochon is oriented toward you. **Split** the stack symmetrically.

11. Pick up a 6 mm bead. Sew up through the stack where the bead hole naturally meets the stack. Make a **one-sided join** (figure 9). With the thread exiting above the join, pick up a 4 mm bead (figure 10) and end the stack.

Figure 9

Figure 10

12. Pull the thread across back of the work and sew through the work so that the thread exits left of the first join. Follow step 11 to make a mirror image (figure 11).

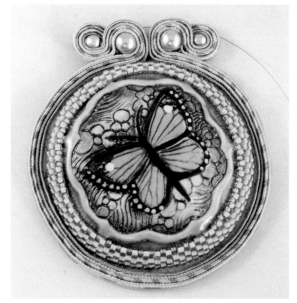

Figure 11

13. Following step 8, create a bridge (figure 12).

Figure 12

14. Prepare a new thread. Cut four 4-inch (10.2 cm) lengths of soutache, one of sage, one of stripe, and two of celery. Align and stack them with sage on the bottom, then celery, stripe, and celery. Sew up through the center of the stack at the ribs. Using the 7 x 12 mm teardrop pearl and being sure to sew through narrow end of the bead first, **make a lollipop** (figure 13). Use **shaping stitches** to consolidate the stack ½ inch (1.3 cm) from the **join**.

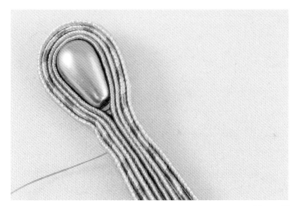

Figure 13

15. Using the remaining four teardrop pearls, repeat step 14 (figure 14).

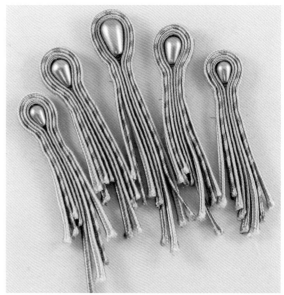

Figure 14

16. Following the directions for **Simple Layered Connections**, center the largest lollipop behind the bottom center of the 55 mm cabochon element. **Tack** it in place (figure 15). Use tacking stitches to attach the medium lollipops to the left and right of the large lollipop. Attach the smallest lollipops left and right of the medium lollipops (figure 16).

Figure 15

Figure 16

17. Add jump rings at the top center of the small cabochon elements (figure 17).

Figure 17

18. Apply backing to all components. Allow the glue to dry completely. **Trim the backing**. Using pearl sage 11° seed beads, **edge bead** each component using **brick stitch edge beading** (figure 18).

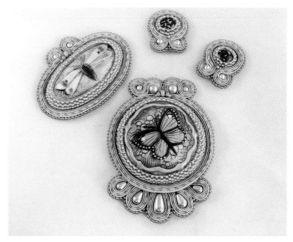

Figure 18

19. Prepare a new thread and **bury the knot** by sewing through the right-hand 4 mm bead of the 55 mm cabochon element and through the stack so that the thread exits the edge beading (figure 19). Sew in and out of the edge beads to work your thread over to the desired connection point (figure 20).

Figure 19

Figure 20

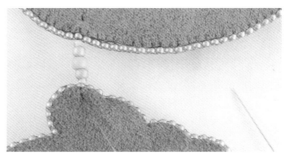

Figure 22

21. To get to next connection point, **surface dive** across the back of the work. Follow step 20 to create a second connection (figure 23).

Figure 23

20. With the thread exiting the desired connection point, pick up a seafoam 11° seed bead, an 8° seed bead, a 6° seed bead, an 8° seed bead, and an 11° seed bead. Sew into the 30 x 55 mm cabochon component at the desired connection point, exiting back through the backing (figure 21). **Retrace the thread path** three times (figure 22).

22. Prepare a new thread. Following steps 19 through 21, connect the smaller cabochon elements above the 30 x 55 mm element (figure 24).

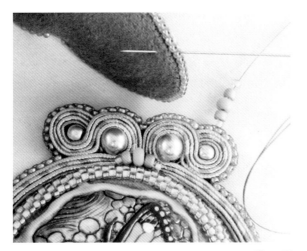

Figure 21

Figure 24

23. Put one 6° seed bead, a 6 mm pearl, and a 6° seed bead on a head pin (figure 25). Following the directions for making a **bead chain**, make a link. Repeat this step to make three more links (figure 26).

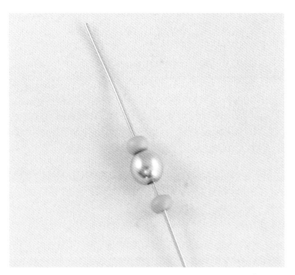

Figure 25

Figure 26

24. Use pliers to open a loop on one of the links. Slip the loop through the end of chain strands (figure 27). Close the loop. Attach a second link to the other end of the chain. Attach one half of the toggle clasp to the other end of that link.

Figure 27

25. Repeat step 24 for the other half of the toggle clasp (figure 28).

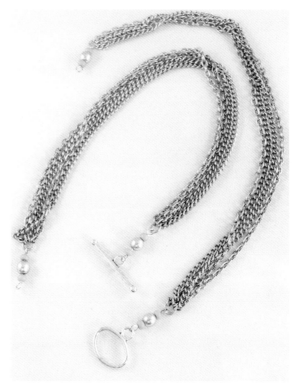

Figure 28

26. Use the pliers to attach the lower links to the jump rings at the top of the soutache elements (figure 29).

Figure 29

Sangria-Style Pin

On a hat, coat, or blazer, this sassy pin is a fiesta waiting to start. There's no one way to put this project together—I encourage you to free yourself up a bit as you attach the components. Think of the curves, ladders, and feathers as naturally growing things, winding around and through one another.

MATERIALS & TOOLS

Beads

Approximately 1¾ x 2¼-inch (4.4 x 5.7 cm)
    shield-shaped polymer clay cabochon

1 g dark copper 8° seed beads

2 g matte gold 11° seed beads

2 g dark copper 11° seed beads

0.5 g silver-lined raspberry 15° seed beads

0.5 g dark copper 15° seed beads

3 topaz 7 x 15 mm navettes with a gold setting

4 6 mm bicone crystals, one each of red AB,
    orange, topaz AB, and rose gold

Soutache

Bead Smith brand ⅛-inch (3 mm) soutache in the
    following amounts and colors:

    2 yards (1.8 m) of beaver brown

    2 yards (1.8 m) of merlot

    2 yards (1.8 m) of ruby glint

    1 yard (91.4 cm) of saffron

    1 yard (91.4 cm) of poinsettia

Brown size B Nymo beading thread

3 x 3-inch (7.6 x 7.6 cm) piece of hawk wing
    Nicole's BeadBacking beading foundation

Craft feathers: 1 red-and-black stripe partridge,
    1 natural guinea, 5 peacock swords,
    1 white rooster fluff, 1 orange rooster coque tail

1½-inch (3.8 cm) gold pin back

4½ x 4½-inch (11.4 x 11.4 cm) piece of tan
    synthetic suede

Size 10 beading needle

Scissors

Washable fiber glue

Jewelry glue

SKILLS USED

Peyote-Stitch Bezel (page 57)

Cabochons (page 57)

Adding Soutache around Beading Foundation
    (page 65)

Making an Independent Curved Ladder
    (page 41)

Add a Pin Backer (page 8)

Layered and Wrapped Connections (page 102)

Edge Beading Negative Spaces (page 91)

Embellished Edges (page 89)

Note: The polymer clay cabochon in this project was made by New Hampshire fine artist Ann Dillon. She is known for her deft handling of color and immaculate finish work.

Steps

Prepare the Cabochon

1. Following the directions for **Cabochons**, glue the cabochon down to the beading foundation. Allow the glue to dry completely. Use matte gold 11° seed beads and silver-lined raspberry 15° seed beads to secure the cabochon with a **peyote-stitch bezel** (figure 1).

Figure 1

2. Prepare the thread. Cut three 18-inch (45.7 cm) lengths of soutache, one each of beaver brown, merlot, and ruby glint. Sew into the back of the beading foundation so the thread exits the center of right, wide side (as viewed from the front with the narrow end down) (figure 2). Locate the center of the beaver brown strand of soutache. Working from the back and following the directions for **Adding Soutache around Beading Foundation**, attach the soutache around the left half of the component, ending at the corner opposite the starting point (figure 3). Attach it around the other side (figure 4). **Align and stack** the merlot and ruby glint strands with the burgundy on the bottom. Attach the stack around the work (figure 5). Join the stacks with a **two-sided join**.

Figure 2

3. With the thread exiting the right side of the join, **train** the large stack to the right. Working from left to right, begin making **invisible shaping stitches** to form the stack into a tight curve (figure 6). Pull the stack behind the work and **tack** it in place (figure 7). Train the stack up and to the left. Consolidate the stack with invisible shaping stitches (figure 8). Pass the end of the working stack through the first loop (figure 9). Tack it in place where the stacks cross (figure 10) and under the work. Trim the thread.

Figure 3

Figure 6

Figure 4

Figure 7

Figure 5

Figure 8

Figure 9

Figure 12

2. Split the stack symmetrically. Sew up through the lower stack on a diagonal so the thread exits about ¼ inch (6 mm) from the **join** (figure 13). Sew through both right holes of navette. Sew through the upper stack (figure 14). Retrace the thread path through the upper stack, the navette, and the lower stack (figure 15). Working from right to left, sew up through the lower stack, the left holes of the navette, and the upper stack. Retrace the thread path (figure 16).

Figure 10

Navette Elements

1. Prepare a new thread. Cut three 12-inch (30.5 cm) lengths of soutache, one each of beaver brown, merlot, and ruby glint. Align and stack them in that order, with the beaver brown on the bottom. Locate the center of the stack. Sew up through the stack at the ribs. Fold the stack over the knot and sew up through all six layers very close to the fold (figure 11). **Retrace the thread path** three times, slightly increasing thread tension with each pass (figure 12).

Figure 13

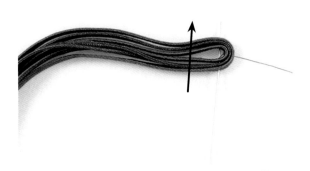

Figure 11

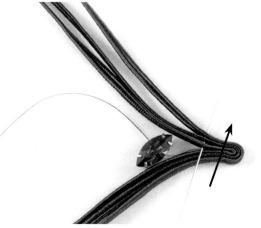

Figure 14

Figure 15

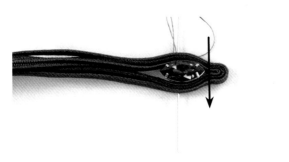

Figure 16

3. Working from right to left, sew through both stacks just beyond the navette (figure 17). Retrace the thread path three times.

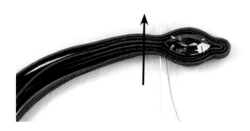

Figure 17

4. Train the working stack into a curve. Working from right to left, consolidate the stack using invisible shaping stitches. (figure 18). Trim the thread.

Figure 18

5. Repeat steps 1 through 4 twice to complete a total of three navette elements (figure 19).

Figure 19

Squiggles

1. Prepare a new thread. Cut two 8-inch (20.3 cm) lengths of soutache, one each of saffron and poinsettia. Align and stack them with saffron on the bottom. Sew up through the center of the stack at the rib. Retrace the thread path (figure 20).

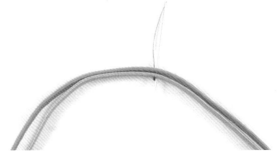

Figure 20

2. Pick up an 8° seed bead. Fold the stack over the knot and bead and sew up through the upper stack. Retrace the thread path (figure 21).

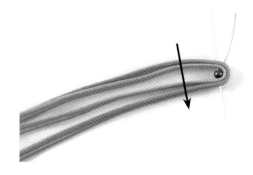

Figure 21

3. Using nine more 8° seed beads, follow the directions for **Making an Independent Curved Ladder** (figure 22). Flip the work over and continue working eight to 10 more 8° seed beads to shape the curve in the opposite direction (figure 23).

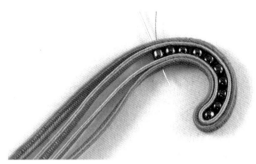

Figure 22

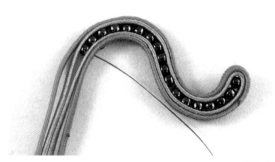

Figure 23

4. Repeat steps 1 through 3 to make another squiggle (figure 24).

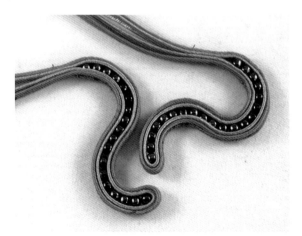

Figure 24

Assembly and Finishing

1. Take a few minutes to play with the shapes you have created, trying out different compositions. (*Psst—there's no right or wrong answer here!*)

2. Once you have a sense of where you want your small elements to connect, begin attaching them to the cabochon component with tacking stitches (figure 25). After an element has been attached, trim off any excess length (figure 26). Continue attaching the elements one at a time, tucking the ends behind the work and allowing the finished shapes to wrap over the front. If you wish, weave them in and out of one another (figures 27 and 28).

Figure 25

Figure 26

Figure 27

Figure 28

3. To work with the craft feathers, put a drop of glue on each of the two larger feathers. Press one or two of the smaller feathers into the glue (figure 29). Allow the glue to dry completely.

Figure 29

4. Slide the quills of the feathers into one of the loops made in the upper corner of the cabochon so the feathers are supported by the loop and the quills are well behind the work (figure 30). Secure in place with tacking stitches that cross over the quills in the back of the work (figure 31).

Figure 30

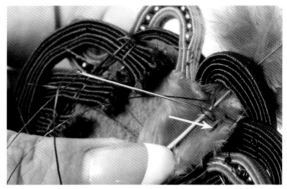

Figure 31

5. If navettes or squiggle ends overlap the cabochon on the front of the work, put a small dab of glue on the cabochon under the element (figure 32). Press the element into the glue and allow it to dry completely.

Figure 32

6. Add the pin back (figure 33).

Figure 33

Sangria-Style Pin **215**

7. Apply backing (figure 34). Allow the glue to dry completely.

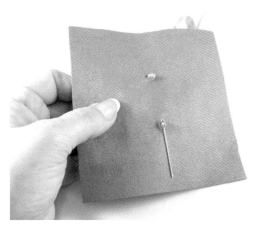

Figure 34

8. Trim the backing.

9. Prepare a new thread. Using dark copper 11° seed beads, **edge bead** using **brick stitch edge beading.** Following the directions for **Edge Beading Negative Spaces**, trim the larger negative spaces with dark copper 15° seed beads (figure 35).

Figure 35

10. Following the directions for **Embellished Edges**, sew through a stack and an edge bead (figure 36). Pick up a dark copper 11° seed bead, a 6 mm bicone, an 11° seed bead, and a 15° seed bead. Sew back through all beads except the 15° seed bead and into the edge beading to make a **fringe** (figure 37). Repeat as desired to make different length fringes, ending with different color bicones (figure 38).

Figure 36

Figure 37

Figure 38

11. Bury the thread and snip it.

Note: Don't happen to have a super-awesome polymer clay cabochon? Think of other smooth, soft-pattern things you could use for a centerpiece: a piece of broken china, stone, glass, plastic, or even fabric stretched over a button.

Dragon Love Necklace

I've always dreamt of having a pet dragon—not a really large one, you understand, but a creature of a more manageable size with a protective-but-pleasant disposition. As that seemed highly unlikely, I decided to make my new pet. I used pivoting/articulating connections that allow his shimmering scales to drape sinuously around my neck.

Materials & Tools

Beads

Rose 10 mm coin pearl

Silver 10 mm coin pearl

2 black 4 mm fire-polished beads

22 silver 4 mm glass pearls

2 burgundy 4 mm glass pearls

18 silver 6 mm glass pearls

15 matte silver 6° seed beads

2 g matte silver 8° seed beads

4 translucent gray 11° seed beads

4 g dark mauve metallic 11° seed beads

2 g silver-lined gray 15° seed beads

8 g purple vitrail SuperDuos

Soutache

ARwS Imported brand ⅛-inch (3 mm) soutache in the following amounts and colors:

    4 yards (3.7 m) black

    4 yards (3.7 m) gray

    3 yards (2.7 m) pewter

    3 yards (2.7 m) celery

    3 yards (2.7 m) delphinium

Dark purple size B Nymo beading thread

2 x 2-inch (5.1 x 5.1 cm) piece of majestic purple beading foundation

3-inch (7.6 cm) length of silver, crystal AB rhinestone chain (6.5 SS)

2 silver 6 mm soldered jump rings

4½ x 9-inch (11.4 x 22.9 cm) piece of eggplant synthetic suede

8 silver 2-inch (5.1 cm) head pins

Toggle clasp

Size 10 beading needle

Scissors

Washable fiber glue

Darning needle

Flat-nose or chain-nose pliers

Looping pliers

Flush cutters

Skills Used

Large Beads: Sew the Bead onto the Foundation (page 55)

Working off the Beading Foundation (page 63)

Adding Soutache around Beading Foundation (page 65)

Making a Lollipop (page 31)

Kissing Connections (page 100)

SuperDuos (page 68)

Flame Stitch (page 50)

Pivoting/Articulating Connections: Method #2 (page 105)

Steps

The Face Component

1. Make the chin element: **Prepare the thread.** Following the directions for **Sew the Bead onto the Foundation**, glue and sew the rose coin pearl to the center of the beading foundation. Following the directions for **Rhinestone Chain**, surround the bead with rhinestone chain (figure 1). **Trim the foundation** (figure 2).

Figure 1

Figure 2

2. Cut three 6-inch (15.2 cm) lengths of soutache, one each of black, gray, and pewter. Following the directions for **Adding Soutache around Beading Foundation**, **make a lollipop** by first attaching the length of black soutache (figure 3). **Align and stack** the remaining two lengths with the gray on the bottom and attach them around the element (figure 4).

Figure 3

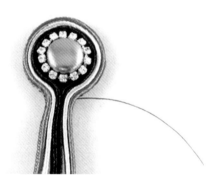

Figure 4

3. Secure the combined stack directly under the **join** by making a few small stitches. Trim the stacks very close to the stitches (figure 5).

Figure 5

4. Make the forehead element: Prepare a new thread. Cut three 4-inch (10.2 cm) lengths of soutache, two of dark gray, one of sage. Align and stack them with the light gray in the middle. Using the silver coin pearl, follow the directions for **Making a Lollipop** (figure 6).

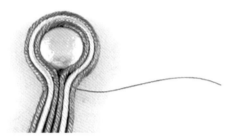

Figure 6

5. With the thread exiting to the right of the join, pick up an 8° seed bead. Cut three 6-inch (15.2 cm) lengths of soutache, two of delphinium and one of black. Align and stack them with the black in the middle. Sew through the working stack 2-inch (5.1 cm) from the right end (figure 7). Working from right to left, use 8° seed beads to make a secured parallel **ladder** around the lollipop (figure 8).

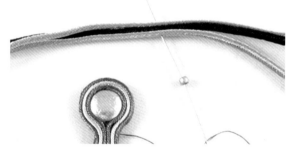

Figure 7

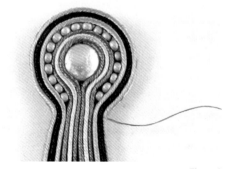

Figure 8

6. Consolidate the combined stack with **shaping stitches** to 1-inch (2.5 cm) below the join. **Set the stitch.** Trim the working stack below the set stitch (figure 9).

Figure 9

7. Make the cheek elements: Prepare a new thread. Cut five 8-inch (20.3 cm) lengths of soutache, one each of black, pewter, delphinium, celery, and gray. Align and stack them in that order with black on the bottom. Using a 4 mm black fire-polished bead, make a lollipop (figure 10).

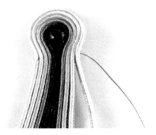

Figure 10

8. Rotate the work so the bead is oriented toward you. With the thread exiting to the right of the join, pick up a 6 mm pearl. **End the stack** and sew through the work so the thread exits left of the join (figure 11).

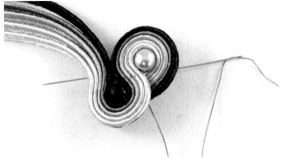

Figure 11

9. Pick up a 6 mm pearl. Sew through the stack where the bead hole naturally meets the stack. Working from right to left and incorporating a silver 4 mm pearl, a 6° seed bead, an 8° seed bead, and a translucent gray 11° seed bead (in that order), make a secured graduated open ladder (figure 12). Set the stitch by **retracing the thread path** twice.

Figure 12

10. Pick up a burgundy 4 mm pearl. Fold the stack back over the bead and sew through the stack where the bead hole naturally meets the stack. End the stack (figure 13).

Figure 13

11. Following steps 7 through 10, make a mirror image (figure 14).

Figure 14

12. Assemble the face: Working from the back, orient the cheek elements so the stacks surrounding the 4 mm burgundy pearls are touching (the 4 mm black fire-polished beads should be facing one another). Make a **kissing connection** between the stacks surrounding the burgundy pearls (figure 15).

Figure 15

13. Place the forehead element behind the cheek elements and **tack** them in place (figure 16). Tack the chin element under the "nose" of the cheek elements and behind the stem of the forehead element (figure 17). Be sure the top few stones of the rhinestone chain are hidden so the resulting curve looks like teeth.

Figure 16

Figure 17

14. Add the whiskers: Cut seven 4-inch (10.2 cm) lengths of gray soutache. Fold one in half and tack the fold behind the center bottom of the chin (figure 18). Repeat with the remaining lengths, one on each side of the center of the chin and two above each "eye" (figure 19).

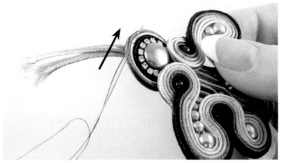

Figure 18

Figure 19

The Body

1. Prepare a new thread. Cut seven 8-inch (20.3 cm) lengths of soutache, one each of gray, sage, and delphinium; two each of black and pewter. Align and stack them with gray on the bottom, then celery, delphinium, black, pewter, gray, and black. Locate the center of the stack and sew up at the rib. Working from left to right, make one shaping stitch (figure 20). Pick up a 6° seed bead. Fold the stack over the bead and knot and sew up through the upper stack (figure 21). Retrace the thread path three times (figure 22). Following the directions for **SuperDuos**, make a 16-SuperDuo motif. Turn the work so the 6° seed bead is oriented toward you. **Split** the stack asymmetrically with six strands going to the left and eight to the right. With the thread exiting right of the join, pick up a 6 mm pearl. Sew up through the stack where the bead hole naturally meets the stack. End the stack. Sew through the work so the thread exits left of the join (figure 23). Pick up a 4 mm silver pearl. Sew up through the stack where the bead hole naturally meets the stack. End the stack (figure 24).

Figure 22

Figure 23

Figure 24

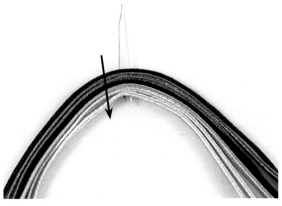

Figure 20

2. Following step 1, make eight more scales of gradually decreasing size (figure 25). Use the chart below to change the size of the remaining eight scales.

Figure 21

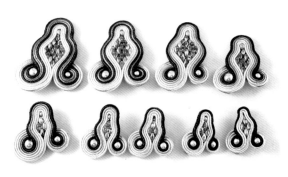

Figure 25

Scale number	Number of lengths of soutache in stack	Measurement of lengths in stack	Color arrangement for stack (the first color is on the bottom) (B = black, P = pewter, D = delphinium, C = celery, G = gray)	Bead at tip of scale	SuperDuo motif	Right-hand bead around which to end stack	Left-hand bead around which to end stack
#2	6	8" (20.3 cm)	G, C, D, B, P, B	6°	16	6 mm	4 mm
#3	5	8" (20.3 cm)	G, C, D, P, B	6°	16	6 mm	4 mm
#4	5	8" (20.3 cm)	G, C, D, P, B	6°	9	6 mm	4 mm
#5	5	6" (15.2 cm)	G, C, D, B	8°	4	6 mm	4 mm
#6	4	6" (15.2 cm)	G, C, D, B	8°	4	6 mm	4 mm
#7	4	6" (15.2 cm)	G, C, D, B	8°	4	4 mm	4 mm
#8	3	6" (15.2 cm)	G, C, B	8°	4	4 mm	4 mm
#9	3	6" (15.2 cm)	G, C, B	None—just fold	4	4 mm	4 mm

3. Add a jump ring to the tip of scale #3 and under the join of scale #4 (figure 26).

Figure 26

The Tail

1. Prepare a new thread. Cut six 12-inch (30.5 cm) lengths of soutache, one each of black, pewter, delphinium, and celery, and two of gray.

2. Align and stack the black and dark gray with the dark gray on the bottom. Sew up through the center of the stack at the ribs. Fold the stack over the knot and sew up through all four layers of braid very close to the fold. Retrace the thread path three times (figure 27).

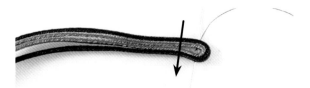

Figure 27

3. Following the directions for **Flame Stitch**, make a curved **graduated ladder** using two dark mauve metallic size 11° seed beads, an 8° seed bead, and a 6° seed bead (figure 28).

Figure 28

4. Following the directions for **Flame Stitch**, add in the next stack of two folded strands, light gray on the inside and lavender (figure 29). Repeat step 3.

Figure 29

5. Repeat step 4 using sage on the inside and light gray (figure 30). Continue the curved ladder, incorporating seven more 6° seed beads (figure 31). Join the large stack. Retrace the thread path three times (figure 32). Trim off the excess soutache (figure 33).

Figure 30

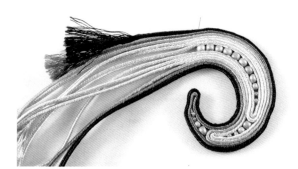

Figure 31

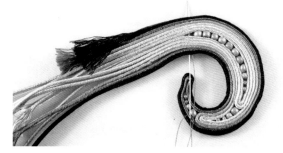

Figure 32

Figure 33

6. With the tip of the tail curving up and to the right, tack the tail behind scale #9 (figure 34).

Figure 34

Finish and Assemble

1. Apply backing to all components. **Trim the backing.** Using dark mauve metallic 11° seed beads and silver-lined gray 15° seed beads, **edge bead** all the components using **brick stitch edge beading**, using the 15° seed beads to embellish with **picots** between every pair of 11° seed beads (figure 35). Be sure to edge bead both the front and back of each of the whisker areas of the face (figure 36).

Figure 35

Figure 36

2. Trim the whiskers to the desired length (figure 37). Drag a darning needle through the rib of each whisker braid to fray it (figure 38).

Figure 37

Figure 38

3. Using 4 mm silver pearls and following the directions for **Pivoting/Articulating Connections: Method #2**, connect scales #1 through #3 and scales #4 through #9. Notice the tip of the larger scale is always on top of the join of the next smaller scale (figure 39). Use the same method to attach the head on top of scale #1 and the tail (figure 40).

Figure 39

Figure 40

4. Put two 8° seed beads and a 6 mm pearl on a head pin. Following the directions for **bead chain**, make a link. Make seven more links (figure 41).

Figure 41

5. Using flat-nose or chain-nose pliers to open and close the loops, connect four links and end with one half of the toggle clasp (figure 42). Repeat with the remaining links and toggle-clasp half (figure 43). Attach the bead chains to jump rings (figure 44).

Figure 42

Figure 44

Note: Making the faces is really fun—minor changes to stack sizes, bead sizes, and angles of connection can dramatically impact the facial expression. There are many ways to embellish the faces and—of course—you can take off on your own and use entirely different techniques (figure 45).

Figure 43

Figure 45

The Tuffet Lily Pendant

Much of the soutache work being made today—
while beautiful—is essentially two-dimensional.
But with a few clever tricks, you can make your
soutache pieces stand up and stand out.
This project will show you three techniques for
bringing three-dimensional qualities to your work.

Materials & Tools

Beads

10 copper 6mm glass pearls

1 g matte translucent yellow 8° AB seed beads

1 g silver-lined clear 8° seed beads

2 g silver-lined gold 11° seed beads

2 g opalescent taupe 11° seed beads

0.5 g silver-lined red 15° seed beads

4 g sage green SuperDuos

4 g brown with half-gold finish SuperDuos

14 gold 4mm glass pearls

Soutache

3 yards (2.7 m) each of BeadSmith brand ⅛-inch (3mm) soutache in the following colors:

    textured metallic bronze

    ivy

    merlot

    maize

    saffron

Burgundy size B beading thread

2 antique brass 6 mm soldered jump rings

4½ x 9-inch (11.4 x 22.9 cm) piece of true red Nicole's BeadBacking beading foundation

4½ x 4½-inch (11.4 x 11.4 cm) piece of green synthetic suede

Size 10 beading needle

Scissors

Washable fiber glue

Skills Used

SuperDuos (page 68)

Steps

The Tuffet

1. Prepare the thread.

2. Cut two 4-inch (10.2 cm) lengths of soutache, one textured metallic bronze and one ivy. Cut one 5-inch (12.7 cm) length of merlot (figure 1). **Align and stack** them with the merlot on the bottom, then textured metallic bronze and ivy. Sew up through the stack approximately 1 inch (2.5 cm) from the right end. **Retrace the thread path twice** (figure 2).

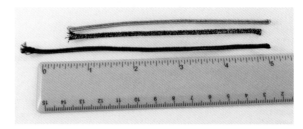

Figure 1

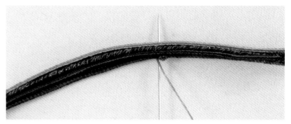

Figure 2

3. Pick up a 6 mm bead.

4. Using the colors in step 2, cut three 4-inch (10.2 cm) lengths of soutache. Align and stack them in the same order. Sew through the new stack 1 inch (2.5 cm) from the right end (figure 3). Pick up another 6 mm bead.

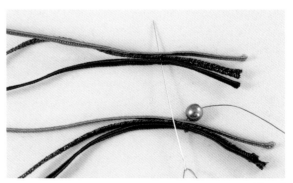

Figure 3

5. Repeat step 4 seven times, alternating stacks and beads. End with a bead. There should be a total of nine stacks and nine beads when complete (figure 4).

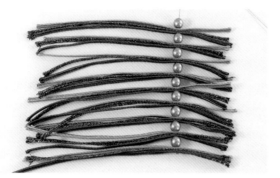

Figure 4

6. Pull the thread back under the line of stacks. Begin sewing through the stacks and beads a second time. The stack with the longer 5-inch (12.7 cm) strand acts as a marker to let you know when you've gone through all the stacks—this is stack 1 (figure 5).

Figure 5

7. Step up by sewing through the stack ⅛ inch (4 mm) from where the thread last exited (figure 6).

Figure 6

8. Pick up a 4 mm bead and sew through the next stack (figure 7).

Figure 7

9. Repeat step 8 until there is a 4 mm bead between each pair of stacks (figure 8). Sew through the stacks and beads a second time to reinforce them.

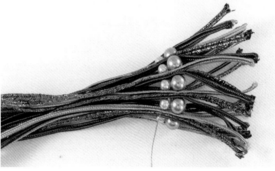

Figure 8

10. Following steps 7 through 9, step up and add a row of silver-lined clear 8° seed beads (figure 9).

Figure 9

11. Following steps 7 through 9, step up and add a row of silver-lined gold 11° seed beads (figure 10).

Figure 10

12. Step up again and sew through the stacks only (figure 11). Sew through stacks a second time, adding thread tension (figure 12).

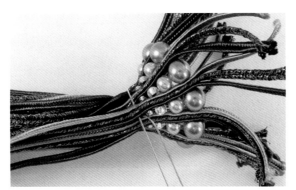

Figure 11

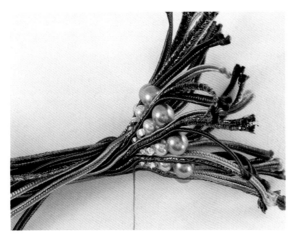

Figure 12

13. Hold the gathered stacks and begin wrapping the thread tightly around them. Sew through the thread and stacks occasionally for reinforcement (figures 13 and 14).

Figure 13

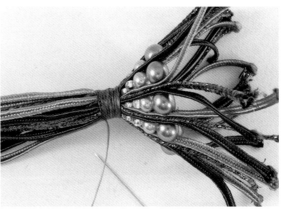

Figure 14

14. Trim the thread. Cut the stacks approximately ½ inch (1.3 cm) beyond the left edge of the thread wraps (figure 15).

Figure 15

15. Gently begin turning the cone inside out, pushing the wrapped nub into the cone. This helps act as stuffing (figure 16).

Figure 16

16. Prepare a new thread and **bury the knot**. Looking at the tuffet from the inside (back), sew through one of the 6 mm beads clockwise so the knot is buried inside the bead. Sew through the stack above the bead (figure 17).

Figure 17

17. Train the stack to the left over the top of the 6 mm bead. Working from right to left, secure the stack in a curve with four **shaping stitches** (figure 18).

Figure 18

18. Wrap the stack over the 6 mm bead and behind the work and **tack** it in place (figure 19).

Figure 19

19. Working from the inside (back) of the work, sew through the stack, the 6 mm bead you just wrapped, and the stack again (figure 20).

Figure 20

20. Working clockwise, sew through next 6 mm bead and next stack (figure 21). Follow steps 17 through 19 (figure 22).

Figure 21

Figure 22

21. Repeat step 20 until each stack is wrapped around the adjacent 6 mm bead and secured to the back of the work (figure 23). Take a few **shallow stitches** in the back of the work (figure 24).

Figure 23

Figure 24

22. Sew up from the back of the work so the thread exits the front of the work in the valley (the small indented point) where all the stacks are gathered (figure 25). Pick up an 8° seed bead and a 15° seed bead. Sew down through the 8° seed bead so the 15° seed bead acts as a stop bead. If the 8° seed bead does not sit firmly in the valley, retrace the thread path through the beads and work (figure 26). Take a couple of shallow stitches in the back of the work and trim thread.

Figure 25

Figure 26

The Small Petals

The following steps will show you how to build a small petal using soutache and SuperDuos. The image shows the order in which the SuperDuos are added. As you are following these instructions, remember when you retrace the thread path that you should add a slight amount of thread tension with each pass (figure 27).

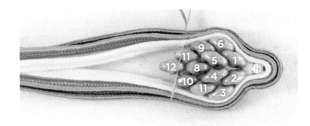

Figure 27

1. Prepare a new thread. Cut three 5-inch (12.7 cm) lengths of soutache, one each of maize, saffron, and ivy. Align and stack them in that order with the maize on the bottom. Sew up through the center of the stack (figure 28).

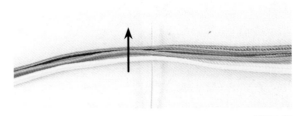

Figure 28

2. Fold the stack over the knot. Bringing the thread around the bottom of the fold, sew up through the lower stack. Pick up a silver-lined clear 8° seed bead and sew through the upper stack (figure 29). Retrace the thread path twice.

Figure 29

3. Working from right to left, sew down through the upper stack one bead width away from where the thread last exited. Pick up two green SuperDuos (SDs). Sew down through the lower stack (figure 30). Retrace the thread path twice.

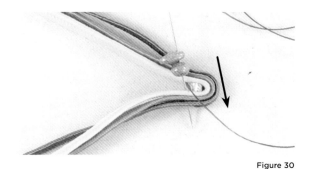

Figure 30

4. Working from right to left, sew up through the lower stack so the thread exits in line with second hole of the second SD. Pick up a third SD. Sew through second hole of the second SD (figure 31).

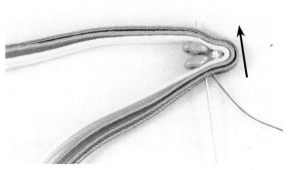

Figure 31

5. Pick up two more SDs. Sew up through second hole of the first SD (figure 32).

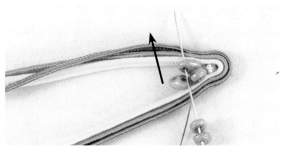

Figure 32

6. Pick up a sixth SD. Sew up through the upper stack (figure 33). Retrace the thread path. The thread should be exiting the lower stack.

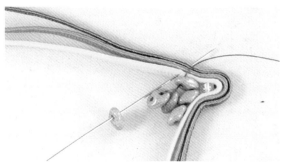

Figure 33

7. Sew up through the lower stack so the thread exits in line with second hole of the third SD. Sew up through the second hole of the third SD (figure 34).

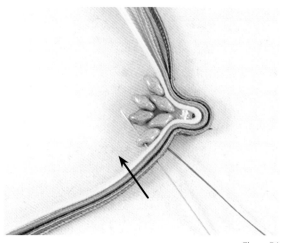

Figure 34

8. Pick up a seventh SD. Sew up through second hole of the fourth SD (figure 35).

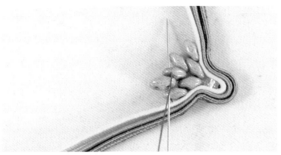

Figure 35

9. Pick up an eighth SD. Sew up through second hole of the fifth SD (figure 36).

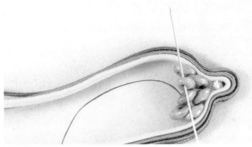

Figure 36

10. Pick up a ninth SD. Sew up through second hole of the sixth SD and the upper stack (figure 37). Retrace the thread path. The thread should be exiting the bottom of the stack (figure 38).

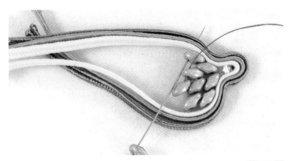

Figure 37

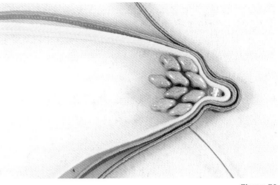

Figure 38

11. Sew up through the bottom of the stack and the second hole of the seventh SD (figure 39). Pick up a 10th SD. Sew up through the second hole of the eighth SD (figure 40).

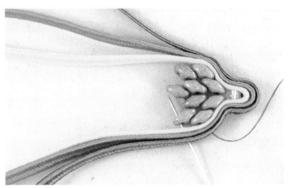

Figure 39

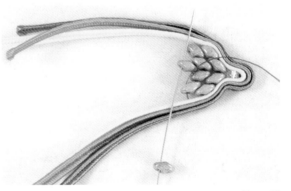

Figure 40

12. Pick up an 11th SD. Sew up through the second hole of the ninth SD and the upper stack (figure 41). Retrace the thread path. The thread should be exiting the bottom stack (figure 42). Notice when thread tension is increased, SDs start to sculpt upward (figure 43).

13. Sew up through the lower stack and the second hole of the 10th SD (figure 44). Pick up a 12th SD and sew up through second hole of the 11th SD (figure 45). Retrace the thread path (figure 46). The thread should be exiting the bottom stack.

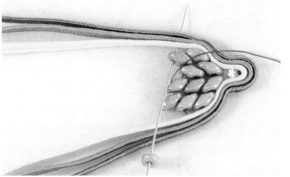

Figure 41

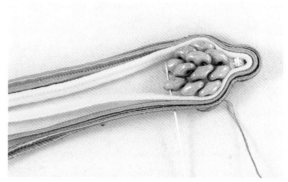

Figure 44

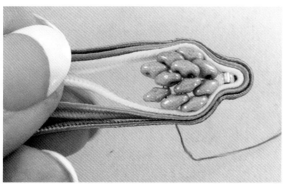

Figure 42

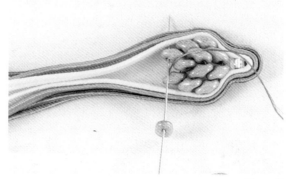

Figure 45

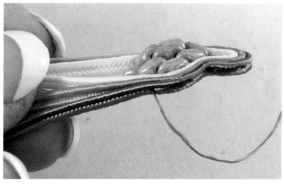

Figure 43

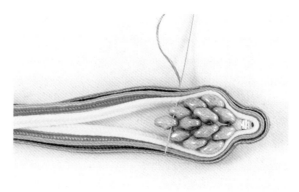

Figure 46

14. Sew up through the bottom stack, the second hole of the 12th SD, and the upper stack. Retrace the thread path (figure 47).

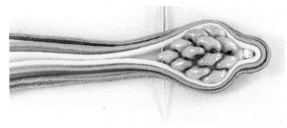

Figure 47

15. Sew up through both stacks. Retrace the thread path (figure 48).

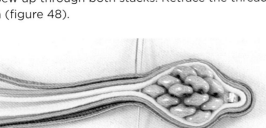

Figure 48

16. Working from right to left, consolidate the large stack with three or four shaping stitches. Trim the thread and the extra soutache (figure 49).

Figure 49

17. Repeat steps 1 through 16 four times to make a total of five small petals (figure 50).

Figure 50

18. Place one of the small petals behind the tuffet. Tack it in place (figure 51). Spacing them evenly, tack the remaining small petals around the tuffet (figure 52).

Figure 51

Figure 52

The Large Petals

Now build the large petals. The image below shows the order in which the SuperDuos and the 4 mm beads are added (figure 53).

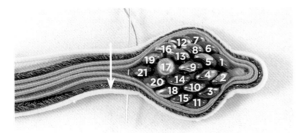

Figure 53

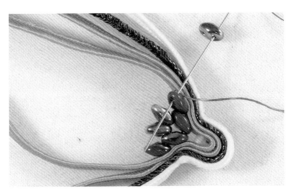

Figure 55

1. Prepare a new thread. Cut four 6-inch (15.2 cm) lengths of soutache, two of saffron, one textured metallic bronze, and one maize. Align and stack them in that order with the saffron on the bottom. Sew up through the center of the stack.

2. Using a translucent yellow 8° seed bead and brown SD, follow the directions for Small Petals, steps 2 through 6. Retrace the thread path one more time so the thread is exiting the upper stack (figure 54).

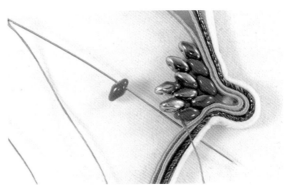

Figure 56

Figure 54

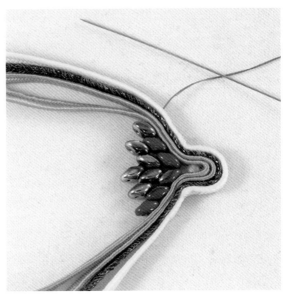

Figure 57

3. Working from right to left, sew down through the upper stack. Following the directions for **SuperDuos Increase**, pick up a seventh SD and sew down through second hole of the sixth SD (figure 55). Add four more SDs, one each between each pair of SDs in row two, ending with an SD between the last SD in row two and the lower stack (figure 56). Retrace the thread path so the thread is exiting the upper stack (figure 57).

4. Working from right to left, sew down through the upper stack and the second hole of 11th SD (figure 58). Working as in **SuperDuos Decrease**, add four more SDs, one each between each pair of SDs in row three. Sew through the lower stack (figure 59). Retrace the thread path so the thread is exiting the upper stack (figure 60).

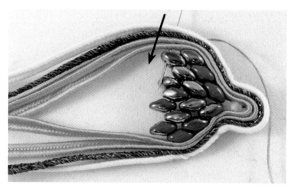

Figure 61

Figure 58

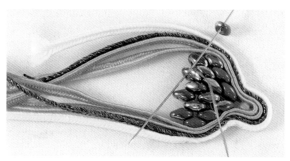

Figure 62

6. Bead 17 is a 4 mm bead. Pick up the 4 mm and sew down through the second hole of the 14th SD (figure 63).

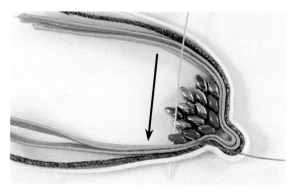

Figure 59

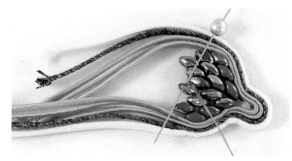

Figure 63

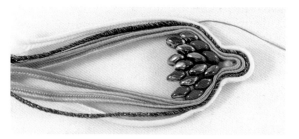

Figure 60

7. Pick up an 18th SD and sew down through the second hole of the 15th SD and the lower stack (figure 64). Retrace the thread path. The thread should be exiting the top of the upper stack (figure 65).

5. Sew down through the upper stack and the second hole of the 12th SD (figure 61). Pick up a 16th SD and sew down through the second hole of the 13th SD (figure 62).

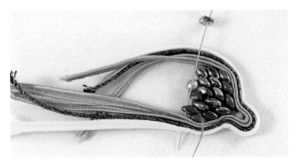

Figure 64

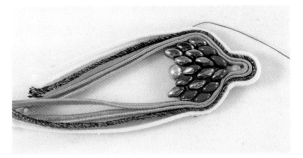

Figure 65

8. Working from right to left, sew down through the upper stack and the second hole of the 16th SD (figure 66). Pick up a 19th SD and sew through the 4 mm bead (figure 67).

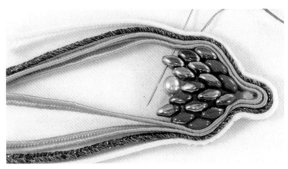

Figure 66

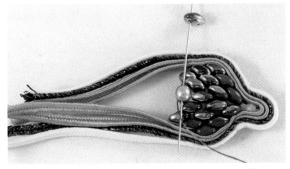

Figure 67

9. Pick up a 20th SD and sew down through the second hole of the 18th SD and the lower stack (figure 68). Retrace the thread path. The thread should exit the top of the upper stack.

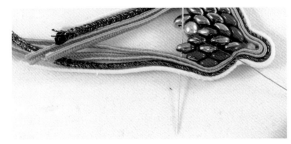

Figure 68

10. Sew down through the upper stack and the second hole of the 19th SD (figure 69). Pick up a 21st SD and sew down through the second hole of the 20th SD and the lower stack (figure 70). Retrace the thread path. The thread should exit the top of the upper stack (figure 71).

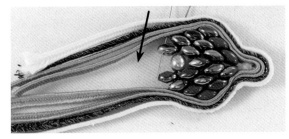

Figure 69

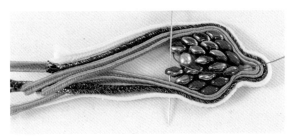

Figure 70

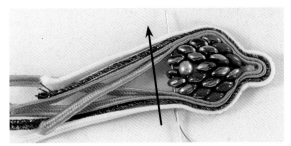

Figure 71

11. Sew down through the upper stack, the second hole of the 21st SD, and the lower stack (figure 72). Retrace the thread path. The thread should be exiting the top of the upper stack (figure 73).

Figure 72

Figure 73

12. Working from right to left, sew down through both stacks. Retrace the thread path (figure 74).

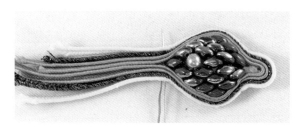

Figure 74

13. Secure the large stack with three or four shaping stitches. Trim the thread and the extra soutache (figure 75).

Figure 75

14. Follow steps 1 through 13 to make four more large petals (figure 76).

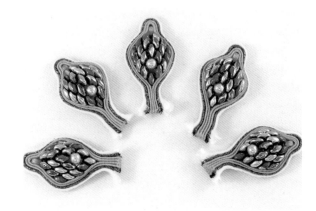

Figure 76

15. Position a large petal behind and between two small petals. Tack it in place (figure 77). Tacks should happen at the stem (figure 78) of the stack as well as through the edges of the widest parts of the petals (figure 79).

Figure 77

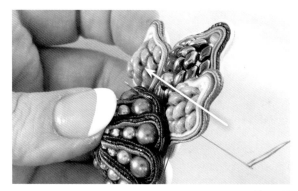

Figure 78

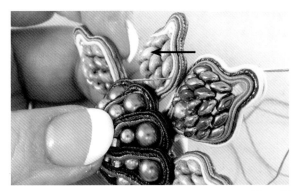

Figure 79

16. Tack the remaining large petals behind each pair of small petals (figure 80).

Figure 80

Assembly and Finishing

1. **Add jump rings** at the tips of the top two large petals (figure 81).

Figure 81

2. Apply the beading foundation: Put a small amount of glue on the back of the work. Keep the glue away from the SuperDuos. Using your fingertip or a toothpick, spread the glue thinly over the back edges of stacks (figure 82). Lay them, glue side down, on the beading foundation. Allow the glue to dry completely.

Figure 82

3. Trim the beading foundation away from work. Leave a thin (1 mm) margin of beading foundation visible beyond the edge of the work (figure 83).

Figure 83

4. Prepare a new thread and bury the knot by sewing into one of the 8° seed beads near the tip of one of the petals and through the stack so the thread exits the rib of the stack outside the work (figure 84). Using silver-lined gold 11° seed beads, **edge bead** using **brick stitch edge beading** (figure 85).

Figure 84

Figure 85

5. Take a shallow stitch in the back of the work and snip the thread (figure 86).

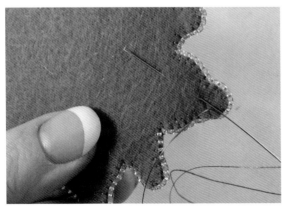

Figure 86

6. Trace the work onto the beading foundation. Mark the locations of the jump rings.

7. Cut the shape out roughly, staying approximately ¼ inch (6 mm) outside the outline (figure 87).

Figure 87

8. Spread a thin layer of glue on the back of the beading foundation (figure 88). Apply the glue side down to the wrong side of the synthetic suede. Allow the glue to dry completely (figure 89).

Figure 88

Figure 89

9. Cut the beading foundation and the synthetic suede shape out along the outline (figure 90).

Figure 90

10. Prepare a new thread. Sew into the beading foundation about ¼ inch (6 mm) from the edge on an angle so the thread exits the suede very close to the edge (figure 91).

Figure 91

11. Using opalescent taupe 11° seed beads, follow step 4. There is no rib to sew into; just sew into the beading foundation very close to the edge (figure 92). **Bury the thread** and snip it.

Figure 92

12. Put a small amount of glue in the center of the beading foundation and synthetic suede shape. Orient the tuffet lily piece to align with the shape and set it in place. Allow to dry completely (figure 93).

Figure 93

13. Connect the layers. Prepare a new thread. Sew into back of the tuffet shape near the point of one of the small petals so the thread exits through the front of the stack (figure 94).

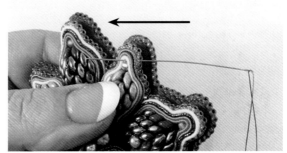

Figure 94

14. Sew through the stack and the edge beading so the thread exits the bead at the center of the tip (figure 95).

Figure 95

15. Pick up a 15° seed bead, an 8° seed bead, and a 15° seed bead.

16. Sew into the corresponding edge bead on the synthetic suede shape (figure 96). The thread should exit the back of the work.

Figure 96

17. Slip stitch just under the synthetic suede and up through the edge bead two beads away from the one the thread last exited (figure 97).

Figure 97

18. Pick up a 15° seed bead, an 8° seed bead, and a 15° seed bead. Sew into the first edge bead to the left of the edge bead on the tuffet lily shape from which the last 15°/8°/15° combination began (figure 98). Sew through the stack.

Figure 98

19. Sew back through the stack and the next edge bead to the left (figure 99). Follow steps 15 and 16. (Note: The 15°/8°/15° combinations are strung through each bead on the tuffet lily layer but are *two beads apart* on the synthetic suede layer) (figure 100).

Figure 99

Figure 100

20. Slip stitch just under the synthetic suede and up through the edge bead two beads to the right of the one anchoring the first connection (figure 101).

Figure 101

21. Follow steps 17 through 19 to make two more connections (figure 102). Bury the thread.

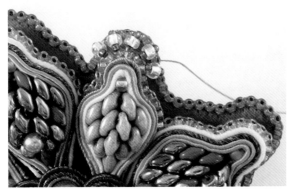

Figure 102

22. Repeat steps 13 through 21 at the tip of each of the remaining four small petals (figure 103).

Figure 103

Note: This piece can be hung on simple strands of ribbon or chain and worn as a pendant or incorporated into much larger, more ambitious pieces of jewelry.

Crazy Quilt Collar

I'm still going to give you the Materials & Tools list,
but it's time to take the training wheels off, so the
list is more generalized. I'll tell you in broad terms
what I used for my example, but I really want you
to think of this less like a project and more of an
independent study. Sure, there are some guidelines,
but they're really more about how to put it together
than a stitch-by-stitch set of instructions.
Don't be scared—you can do this. Let's begin.

Materials & Tools

Beads

Remember this is a suggested list. If you don't have everything on it, don't let it slow you down. Either substitute or forget it and move on.

2 or 3 large beads (10 to 25 mm), any kind

10 to 20 6 mm round beads (any two colors)

10 to 20 4 mm round beads (any two colors)

10 to 20 6 mm fire-polished beads (any two colors)

10 to 20 4 mm fire-polished (any two colors)

10 to 20 6 mm bicone crystals (any two colors)

20 to 30 4 mm bicone crystals (any two colors)

2 grams SuperDuo beads (any color)

2 to 4 g 6° seed beads (any two colors)

2 to 4 g 8° seed beads (any two colors)

2 to 6 grams 11° seed beads (any two colors)

1 gram 15° seed beads (any color)

2-inch (5.1 cm) or smaller chandelier crystal

Soutache

5 yards (4.6 m) each of ARwS imported ⅛-inch (3 mm) soutache in eight or so different colors (I used rose, dusty rose, fuchsia, orange, rust, wine, royal blue, and turquoise)

Size B beading thread (any color)

1 6-inch (15 cm) length of shibori silk ribbon (any color)

4½ x 9-inch (11.4 x 22.9 cm) piece of foundation

4½ x 9-inch (11.4 x 22.9 cm) piece of synthetic suede (any color)

Jump rings

8-inch (20.3 cm) length of 6.5 SS rhinestone chain

2 or 3 brass 1-inch (2.5 cm) soldered hoops

Toggle clasp

Size 10 beading needle

Scissors

Washable fabric glue

Flat-nose or chain-nose pliers

Looping pliers

Flush cutter

Permanent marker

Tape

Skills Used

Everything!

Steps

1. Gather your materials. I recommend starting with your soutache. From there, start pulling out a wide variety of beads, cabochons, chain, crystals—whatever you feel works with the colors you've selected. Don't be overly critical and—for heaven's sake—don't waste a lot of time *dithering* over this! Too much great work is lost to overthinking. Make your selections, stick your chin in the air, and march forward with confidence.

2. Sort and organize your materials onto a tray or other surface (figure 1). This is a good time to do a little editing. If you have five tubes of 11° seed beads clutched in your little paw, put two or three back. Part of what is going to make this project work (and I promise you, it *will* work) is having certain elements repeat themselves throughout the piece—too many varieties of the same material and you'll lose cohesiveness.

Figure 1

3. Now—*MAKE STUFF.* Make *LOTS* of stuff. Don't censor yourself and don't worry about where this or that is going to go on the finished piece. Use as many techniques from this book as you like and—most of all—*enjoy yourself!* Think of each little component you make as an individual work of art. Depending on how large you want your necklace to be, make some pieces one-half to three-quarters the size of your palm. Make many smaller ones. And lots of **lollipops**—don't forget those, they're going to be very helpful later. Accept the fact that you might not use every single piece in this necklace, and that's OK; they can always grow up to be something else later (figure 2). Don't back or edge bead most of these yet.

Figure 2

4. Print out the circular necklace template on page 257. Eyeball the line you think might be just a little smaller than you want the inside neck hole of your necklace-to-be. Cut it out at that point (figure 3) and try it on in front of a mirror (figure 4). Need the neck hole a little bigger? Trim another line or two down.

Figure 3

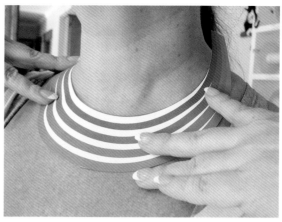

Figure 4

5. Begin arranging some of the larger pieces on top of your template. Experiment until you like the composition (figure 5).

Figure 5

6. Once you have the foundation of your design, take note of any spaces between the components and the top (inside the neckline) and bottom of your necklace (figure 6).

Figure 6

7. Tack smaller elements and lollipops behind the components to enlarge them to better fill the empty areas (figure 7).

Figure 7

8. Add jump rings to the top points of the necklace where you want to attach neck straps (figure 8).

Figure 8

9. Apply backing to all components individually (figure 9). I used two colors of backing because I kind of get a kick out of it when the back of the necklace is just as much fun as the front.

Figure 9

10. Trim the backing. Edge bead all the components using **brick stitch edge beading** (figure 10).

Figure 10

11. Lay the components back on template in the desired arrangement (figure 11). Put a small loop of tape under each component to keep it from sliding around (figure 12).

Figure 11

Figure 12

12. Prepare a new thread and **bury the knot** by sewing through one of the larger beads in a component so the thread exits the edge beading (figure 13).

Figure 13

13. Pick up a line of seed beads (figure 14). Compare the line against the distance between this component and the adjacent one and add or subtract beads to fit. Sew through the adjacent component at the edge beading (figure 15). **Retrace the thread path** to reinforce the connection.

Figure 14

Figure 15

14. Trace a path to exit another edge bead (figure 16).

Figure 16

15. Following steps 13 and 14, create a web of connections between the components, occasionally exiting the connection strand at the midway point and branching off in a different direction (figures 17 and 18).

Figure 17

Figure 18

16. Take the work off the template and inspect it. Are all the connections snug? Do there seem to be any holes that need filling in (figure 19)?

Figure 19

17. If you have what feels like an empty spot (figure 20), follow the directions for **Embellished Edges** to add visual weight to that area (figure 21).

Figure 20

Figure 21

18. Make bead chain to the desired length and add a toggle clasp.

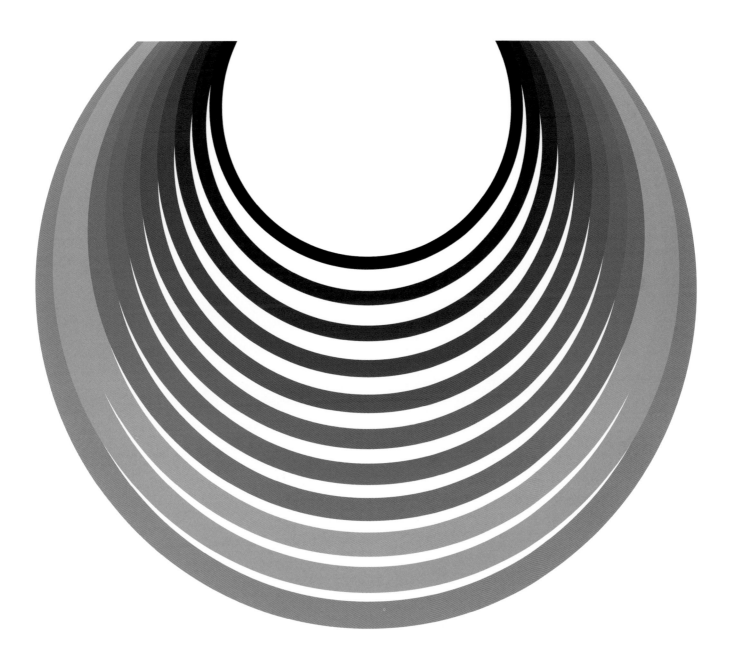

Copy at 125%

RESOURCES

The Art of Bead Embroidery by Heidi Kummli and Sherry Serafini

Dimensional Bead Embroidery: A Reference Guide to Techniques by Jamie Cloud Eakin

Kumihimo Basics and Beyond: 24 Braided and Beaded Jewelry Projects on the Kumihimo Disk by Rebecca Combs

"Serpents, Splashes & Swans' Heads" necklace in "Hopscotch"
Model: Maureen Szewczyk
Photo: Photography by Nylora

"Chain, Chain, Chain" necklace in "Snow Angel"
Model: Donna E. Sweet
Photo: Photography by Nylora

"Chapeau for Leo" hat with embellishment.
Model: Caryn M. Wells
Photo: Photography by Nylora

"Cleopatra's Cavalry" earrings and cuff
Model: Rana Shine
Photo: Pam Jones Photography

ABOUT THE AUTHOR

Ask **Amee K. Sweet-McNamara** why her fine-art jewelry business is called "Amee Runs with Scissors," and she usually just laughs and says, "Because it sounds a whole lot sexier than 'Amee Eats Paste.'"

Working out of her southern New Hampshire home, Sweet-McNamara makes one-of-a-kind pieces of wearable-art textile jewelry using soutache and bead embroidery, which involves hand-stitching yards and yards of soutache braid and hundreds of tiny beads. She is inspired by curvilinear shapes and unexpected color combinations wherever she discovers them; fine art, movies, architecture, or advertising. Sweet-McNamara writes books, contributes to craft magazines, sells her work through galleries and craft shows, teaches both private and group classes nationally and internationally, and is a proud member of the League of New Hampshire Craftsmen.

Index

Note: Page numbers in *italics* indicate projects.